# HE'S NOT WHO YOU THINK HE IS

*Dropping Your Assumptions and Discovering God for Yourself*

Russ Ewell

Sunnyvale, CA

*He's Not Who You Think He Is: Dropping Your Assumptions and Discovering God for Yourself* Copyright © 2022 Deep Spirituality LLC

All rights reserved. No part of this book may be used or reproduced in any manner whatsoever without written permission from Deep Spirituality LLC.

To request permissions, email info@deepspirituality.com.

Originally published in 2010 as *When God Isn't Attractive: An Innovative Guide to Developing an Inspiring Relationship with God.*

Written by Russ Ewell.
Cover and interior design by J.R. Caines of Caines Design.
Illustrations by Olivia Le Brun.
Copyediting by Christina Pfister of Well Versed Edits and Translations.

Paperback: 979-8-9854812-0-4
E-Book: 979-8-9854812-1-1
Audiobook: 979-8-9854812-2-8

All Scripture quotations, unless otherwise indicated, are taken from the Holy Bible, New International Version®, NIV®. Copyright ©1973, 1978, 1984, 2011 by Biblica, Inc.™ Used by permission of Zondervan. All rights reserved worldwide. www.zondervan.com. The "NIV" and "New International Version" are trademarks registered in the United States Patent and Trademark Office by Biblica, Inc.™

Scripture quotations marked (NLT) are taken from the Holy Bible, New Living Translation, copyright ©1996, 2004, 2015 by Tyndale House Foundation. Used by permission of Tyndale House Publishers, Carol Stream, Illinois 60188. All rights reserved.

Scripture quotations marked MSG are taken from THE MESSAGE, copyright © 1993, 2002, 2018 by Eugene H. Peterson. Used by permission of NavPress, represented by Tyndale House Publishers. All rights reserved.

Underlined words in Bible quotations indicate the emphasis of the author.

Printed in the United States of America.

**deepspirituality.com**

# DEDICATION

*For Ethel Ewell and Nancy Butterfield.*
*Your lives have made a difference.*

# TABLE OF CONTENTS

| | |
|---|---|
| **PREFACE TO THE SECOND EDITION** | VII |
| **A NOTE TO OUR READERS** | XIII |
| **INTRODUCTION** | XV |
| **CHAPTER ONE: WHEN GOD ISN'T ATTRACTIVE** | |
| *Turning Unhealthy Thoughts into Healthy Ones* | 21 |
| **CHAPTER TWO: WHEN RELIGION BECOMES GOD** | |
| *Understanding the Difference Between God and Religion* | 41 |
| **CHAPTER THREE: WHEN PEOPLE BECOME GOD** | |
| *Overcoming the Fear of Being Different* | 54 |
| **CHAPTER FOUR: WHEN EMOTIONS BECOME GOD** | |
| *Increasing Our Emotional Awareness* | 73 |
| **CHAPTER FIVE: WHY WE DOUBT GOD** | |
| *Identifying Our Unfinished Emotional Business* | 89 |
| **CHAPTER SIX: HOW GOD BECOMES SATISFYING** | |
| *Rebuilding Our Emotional Lives* | 106 |
| **CHAPTER SEVEN: WHAT MAKES GOD ATTRACTIVE** | |
| *How We Can Change the World* | 124 |
| **CHAPTER EIGHT: PRACTICAL STEPS FOR MAKING GOD ATTRACTIVE** | |
| *How to Develop Your Own Unique Relationship with God* | 153 |
| **ENDNOTES** | 184 |

# PREFACE TO THE 2022 EDITION

> Then some Pharisees and teachers of the law came to Jesus from Jerusalem and asked, "Why do your disciples break the tradition of the elders? They don't wash their hands before they eat!" Jesus replied, "And why do you break the command of God for the sake of your tradition?"
>
> Matthew 15:1–3

There is something deeply disturbing about the discovery that what you were against is what you are becoming. This was my realization in a conversation in which I felt increasing pressure to conform to a set of religious principles more associated with the politics and power-seeking of organized religion than the spirituality and authenticity of biblical Christianity.

Those with whom I spoke had clearly ignored or dismissed the content of my book *When God Isn't Attractive: An Innovative Guide to Developing an Inspiring Relationship with God*. If they had taken it seriously—and all of them had received a copy—they would have realized that chapter 2, "When Religion Becomes God," was my declaration of independence from ritualistic religion. It was my decision to return to what had inspired me to become a Christian: the passionate pursuit of God and the mission to make him known, rather than the building of an organization to make it or myself known.

Since that conversation, I have deepened my commitment to God and making him known. Recent conversations of the same type mentioned above have reminded me how easy it is to equate religious traditions, past assumptions, and personal preferences with the actual Word of God. In so doing, we make God inaccessible to those who do not share our tastes.

Discussing all of this with my circle of advisers, which includes family, friends, mentors, as well as the Deep Spirituality team, it seemed appropriate to release an updated version of my book with a new title: *He's Not Who You Think He Is: Dropping Your Assumptions and Discovering God for Yourself.*

## WHY SHOULD I READ THIS BOOK?

> No one has ever seen God, but the one and only Son, who is himself God and is in closest relationship with the Father, has made him known.
>
> John 1:18

You should read this book whether you are convinced or merely curious about how God can work in our lives individually or as a community. This book is for you if you have been disturbed, unsettled, or even made cynical by religion in general or Christianity in particular. While I do not consider my spiritual education complete, this book represents an effort to break through the encumbrances and entanglements Jesus never intended to get in the way of us knowing God.

Jesus was a simple man with a simple plan to make God known. This truth eluded me for decades, until the aforementioned conversations when I realized that my religiosity was limiting my capacity to see and understand the Christianity described in the Bible.

The Cambridge Dictionary defines religiosity as "the quality of being very or too religious, or reminding you of religious behavior, often in a way that is annoying."¹ We see religiosity on full display in the lives of the Pharisees.

> "Woe to you, teachers of the law and Pharisees, you hypocrites! You clean the outside of the cup and dish, but inside they are full of greed and self-indulgence. Blind Pharisee! First clean the inside of the cup and dish, and then the outside also will be clean."
>
> Matthew 23:25-26

The Pharisees of Jesus' day demonstrated a religiosity which was outward and behavioral only. They did not internalize their faith. For them, everything was about appearances and performing rather than believing and living their faith authentically from the inside out.

> "Everything they do is done for people to see: They make their phylacteries wide and the tassels on their garments long; they love the place of honor at banquets and the most important seats in the synagogues; they love to be greeted with respect in the marketplaces and to be called 'Rabbi' by others."
>
> Matthew 23:5-7

These Pharisees turned the experience of God into a burden (Matthew 23:1-4 NLT), creating a ritualistic religion that emphasized rules rather than relationship (Colossians 2:20-23, 1 Corinthians 8:1-3 NIV).

The writing in this book is an attempt to replace the burdensome practice of pharisaical Christianity with the spiritual experience of knowing God and making him known, to discover the Christianity Jesus intended, those inspiring and innovative communities of faith found in the New Testament, filled with people who know both how to walk with God and make him accessible to others.

## HOW TO READ THIS BOOK

> They read from the Book of the Law of God, making it clear and giving the meaning so that the people understood what was being read.
>
> Nehemiah 8:8

In 2010, pen touched paper in my pursuit of freedom from the religiosity which had come to permeate my life. The result was the first edition of this book, which I called *When God Isn't Attractive: An Innovative Guide to Developing an Inspiring Relationship with God*. What I didn't explain then was how to read this book.

This book is to be read spiritually. It is not a how-to guide, describing how to live your life or build a ministry, but a sanctuary for your heart, mind, and soul. It is a place of discovery, where you can let go of your assumptions and learn to think differently about your walk with God—or even your church.

I was tempted to rewrite the book completely instead of updating it. But then I realized, this book is not sacred. It is merely an effort to share my process for changing how I think about God and his church. I write from the point of view of trusting the authority of the Bible, and throughout this book I've added emphasis to specific words and phrases from passages of Scripture that have influenced and shaped my thinking.

## PREFACE TO THE SECOND EDITION

For me, the results of changing the way I think have been stunning, not because the book taught me what to do, but because the experience of writing it taught me how to think spiritually.

My hope is that you will experience the same transformation of thought that changed my life, a change best captured by an article I published on one of the initiatives that came from this change.

> What this journey has meant to me, even writing this article, is to set me free to write as I must to fulfill the truth of my journey. I am not one thing—entrepreneur, writer, pastor, spiritual theologian, inclusion advocate, technologist, applied historian, thought leader—but I am many things all coming together with the march forward of each year lived in pursuit of discovery, the discovery of my voice. [2]

We are all complicated people whose potential lies in breaking free from every obstacle, encumbrance, entanglement, and human limitation that keeps us too insecure to run our race (1 Corinthians 9:24–27 NLT, Hebrews 12:1 NLT). Read on and let God inspire you to believe in and pursue the destiny for which he has chosen you to live so that you may make him known.

# A NOTE TO OUR READERS

When the first edition of this book was published in 2010, the idea of using innovative digital tools and media to build an inspiring relationship with God was, well, really just an idea.

At that time, one of the most cutting-edge, non-traditional Bible reading experiences was buying a DVD Bible or finding a 1979 movie about Jesus.

Thankfully, technology has come a long way, and so have we. In 2017, Deep Spirituality was born. This site is home to a vast and growing library of spiritual content, including hundreds of devotionals, videos, podcast episodes, and music playlists. Our vision is that Deep Spirituality will provide instant access to everything you need to build a rich relationship with God, no matter where in the world you are located.

This book, originally written in 2010 by the Deep Spirituality Editor-In-Chief, Russ Ewell, has been personally transformative to each of us. We were excited to give it a fresh upgrade, complete with new, dynamic content.

The second edition offers a full multimedia experience. Throughout the pages, you'll find:

- **Interactive Media:** A scan with your phone's camera will take you to related devotionals, podcasts, and videos from Deep Spirituality, so you can bring ideas from the book into your own Bible study.
- **Visual Journal Pages:** Each chapter ends with a visual reflection guide to help you process the themes

discussed. Take notes, doodle, or double back on the Scripture passages referenced.
- **Music Playlists:** Throughout the book, we included curated collections of music designed to help you experience a deeper emotional connection with God.

We love this book and it has revolutionized the way we think about God. We hope you enjoy the experience of getting to know God better as much as we have!

**The Deep Spirituality Team**
*Sunnyvale, CA*
*August 2022*

# INTRODUCTION

And they were all amazed at the greatness of God.

Luke 9:43

There are moments in life when everything changes—breakthroughs so powerful they render the past irrelevant and the present obsolete. These moments open our eyes to a new way of thinking and living so profound that we will never be the same. This is the experience of those who come to understand the greatness of God.

I remember watching a boy named Charlie experience this moment at sixteen. Charlie saw little need for God. He was popular, talented, and satisfied. There was little he wanted that he couldn't easily get. He possessed a humorous cynicism that disguised a philosophical curiosity. This curiosity gave me a sense that Charlie was looking for God, even if he didn't know it.

One day, while hanging with Charlie and some of his friends, a question with breakthrough potential occurred to me. I asked, "Charlie, did your best friend's death at sixteen have any effect on how you feel about God?" His response was honest and revealing. Charlie said, "Yeah, I think so. I guess I blame God for letting him die. If God is good and great, then why did he let Jeff die?"

Charlie isn't that different from the rest of us. He said he wasn't interested in God or "the whole religion thing" because he found it boring and less than useful in his everyday life. What he had not revealed, or even been aware of himself, was that events had changed his view of God. Life had made God unattractive for Charlie and nothing would change until he could begin to know God for who he was rather than who he appeared to be. This was my quest with Charlie and it is the same for you as you read this book. I want to help you know God for who he is, not for who he appears to be.

## CHANGE YOUR FUTURE

Hope depends upon our belief that the future can be changed. We can examine the past, learn from it, and make decisions that will alter the course of our life. This is exactly how Charlie changed his view of God and as a result changed his life. He had to look at what had happened before he could understand what was happening.

This is what we have to do when God is unattractive to us. In a sense, we have to discover what it is that made us stop seeing God as great. We have to look back, so we can learn how to move forward and direct our future.

## BECOME INSPIRED

> For you have been my hope, Sovereign Lord, my confidence since my youth. From birth I have relied on you; you brought me forth from my mother's womb. I will ever praise you.
>
> Psalm 71:5-6

My earliest impressions of God are from a dream I had. In this dream, God was a big kid, wearing a striped T-shirt. God was my playmate, friend, and big brother. He was the older kid who became like a little kid to hang with his younger brother. I liked this view of God, but it has been a difficult one to sustain.

The years have taught me that our early and innocent views of God can be damaged, distorted, or destroyed. Those occasions when I felt God had punished me too hard, left me unprotected, or failed to give me what I needed damaged my view of God. I stopped trusting him.

Moments when I placed too much importance on pleasing people distorted my understanding of who God was and what he wanted from me. I listened more to what people said about God than to what he said about himself in the Bible. My view of God was based on assumptions and misconceptions, rooted in religious tradition rather than in the truth of the Bible.

Even before my relationship with God could be damaged or distorted, it was almost destroyed during my middle school and teen years. I began to think that God and the practice of Christianity were about the pursuit of the good rather than the pursuit of the great.

> Good is the enemy of great. And that is one of the key reasons why we have so little that becomes great.
>
> —Jim Collins[3]

I never wanted a good life. I have always wanted a *great* life. Sometimes these ambitions were selfish and at other times they were unselfish, but in every case I wanted to do something great. The only failure in life I could fathom was being ordinary, typical, or forgettable.

Growing up in the late '60s and '70s, I was surrounded by living history. The memories my parents shared with me and the events to which I was exposed were of greatness. They were of John F. Kennedy, Martin Luther King, and Robert F. Kennedy. The fight for justice and the rights of oppressed people were constantly in the headlines. The fight against corruption was exemplified by Watergate. The music of Bob Dylan, Marvin Gaye, and the collective voices of Woodstock brought meaning and a voice to the pain and passion of people who wanted to make a difference in the world. The world in which I was coming of age seemed to have potential for greatness at every corner. And then there was church.

Church was merely good, not great. As a result, that was how I saw God. God was good, but he wasn't great—which made it difficult for me to want a relationship with him. I wanted to do *great* things with my life, and from what I could tell, God would only get in the way.

> You make your saving help my shield, and your right hand sustains me; your help has made me great.
>
> Psalm 18:35

Until I could see that God was great, Christianity wasn't attractive to me. I didn't have time for or interest in a God who was boring, uninvolved, or lacking ambition. This is why I didn't give God a second thought until I met people who saw God as great. These people weren't satisfied to be religious churchgoers, wrapped up in old-fashioned traditions. They were exciting rather than boring. They weren't stuck in the past but focused on the future. They weren't ordinary, typical, or forgettable. They wanted to change the world.

When God is unattractive, we have allowed something or someone to distract us from the truth about him. This doesn't mean we can blame other people. Our view of God is our own responsibility. We have to make certain that what we believe about God is true.

Before my friend Charlie and I could find out the truth about God, we had to experience breakthroughs and discoveries. The same is true for anyone who wants a healthy and inspiring relationship with God. In fact, anyone who wants this type of relationship with God will have to, along with Charlie and me, devote his or her whole life to this pursuit.

What about you? What kind of relationship with God do you have? What kind of relationship with God do you want? Are you willing to tackle the core reasons why you might find God unattractive and change those views? Can you expand your imagination and dream of a God who is both irresistible and attractive? Don't be afraid. Keep reading—let's begin!

**Russ Ewell**
*San Francisco, California 2010*

## Chapter 1
# WHEN GOD ISN'T ATTRACTIVE

*Turning Unhealthy Thoughts into Healthy Ones*

> No one can serve two masters. Either you will hate the one and love the other, or you will be devoted to the one and despise the other. You cannot serve both God and money.
>
> Matthew 6:24

The Bible teaches that you can't serve both God and money. While that is very true, there is no question that there are times when money can make God quite attractive. Let me explain what I mean by giving you an example from my own life.

I loved high school. I am not sure anyone I knew then will remember things in the same way that I do, but my recollection is that I had some pretty good friends. One of those friends was Jeff Shipman. He was the first guy who ever inspired me to attend a religious event of my own accord. You might say he was the first person to make God attractive to me.

He was a member of a popular Christian student group in our high school. A number of my friends attended their

Wednesday night gathering and other activities. I had never attended and did all I could to avoid the leader of the group.

As I mentioned in the introduction, I saw God and religion as good. But I wanted to be great, so I wouldn't be caught dead in church or anything resembling it. This remained true until Jeff came to me with a deal of sorts.

Jeff told me, "Hey Russ, you should come to our club meeting next Wednesday night." Now, Jeff knew that my only religion was the worship of my grades, my basketball, and myself, so I wondered why he would present this invitation to me, of all people.

My face clearly reflected the stress of a person whose religious friend has him cornered. Jeff moved in for the kill. To close the deal, he said, "You should come. Whoever brings a friend gets their name entered into a contest to win twenty dollars."

I replied with no small amount of emotion, "Twenty dollars!" My face now reflected the joy of a person who just figured out how to fill up his gas tank for a week (at least in 1979). I agreed enthusiastically and was on my way to attending my first religious event since elementary school.

Jeff made the event attractive to me. For the record, we did win that contest. After a little conflict, we split the $20 evenly between us. Unfortunately, I never returned to that student group or any other religious event during my teen years. Why? My attraction hadn't been to God, but to the money. I still found God unattractive.

## WHEN GOD ISN'T ATTRACTIVE

When God isn't attractive to us, there isn't a gimmick on earth that can motivate us to seek him. Rather than relying on a gimmick to make God attractive, we have to discover and deal with the root of our disinterest, dislike, or downright repulsion. That root usually has something to do with how we see God and whether we have healthy (productive) or unhealthy (destructive) thoughts about him.

Jesus taught us about a man who had such a problem:

> Again, it will be like a man going on a journey, who called his servants and entrusted his wealth to them. To one he gave five bags of gold, to another two bags, and to another one bag, each according to his ability. Then he went on his journey. The man who had received five bags of gold went at once and put his money to work and gained five bags more. So also, the one with two bags of gold gained two more. But the man who had received one bag went off, dug a hole in the ground and hid his master's money.
>
> Matthew 25:14-18

Imagine yourself as the man in the passage who received the one bag of gold. God gave the first man five bags of gold, the next man two bags, and last of all you get one. How does that make you think and feel about God?

You might find yourself thinking things like:

- "He isn't fair!"
- "Who is he to judge?"
- "You call this love?"
- "Do you know how to build anything other than a master/slave relationship?"

All of these are reasonable reactions. So, how did the servant in the story react?

1. He went off.
2. He dug a hole.
3. He hid his master's money.

Have you ever felt like this man? Have you ever felt that God valued other people more than he valued you? Have you ever felt that God blessed others while he ignored you? Have you ever felt that he was unfair to you? Have you ever felt that he mistreated you? How have you reacted negatively to these feelings?

The servant was clearly angry, as any of us might have been. His actions seemed to say, "Humph, how dare you only consider me worth one bag!" His response and attitude were very different from the servant who received five bags. How did the servant who received five bags of gold react?

1. He went out at once.
2. He put the money to work.
3. He gained five more bags.

As we will see, it wasn't the amount of gold the servants received that shaped their reactions, but rather their underlying view of and attitude toward God. The servant with five bags had a healthy view of God, while the servant with one had an unhealthy view. It is not surprising that it was the latter servant who viewed God as unattractive.

This is the question we have to ask ourselves: "Have my feelings toward and reactions to God become negative because I have an unhealthy view of him?"

## A HEALTHY VIEW OF GOD

> After a long time the master of those servants returned and settled accounts with them. The man who had received five bags of gold brought the other five. "Master," he said, "you entrusted me with five bags of gold. See, I have gained five more." His master replied, "Well done, good and faithful servant! You have been faithful with a few things; I will put you in charge of many things. Come and share your master's happiness!" The man with two bags of gold also came. "Master," he said, "you entrusted me with two bags of gold; see, I have gained two more." His master replied, "Well done, good and faithful servant! You have been faithful with a few things; I will put you in charge of many things. Come and share your master's happiness!"
>
> Matthew 25:19–23

We can see from the very beginning of the story that the five-bag and two-bag servants had a very different reaction from the one-bag servant. As we read further, we are given an insight into the motivation behind their responses.

The master in the story says that both the five-bag and two-bag servants have been faithful, and he offers them the opportunity to share in his happiness. The word "faithful" is similar to the word "loyal." It is a relationship word—a very powerful relationship word. The word "share" is another powerful relationship word. It is an expression of trust, even intimacy.

The lesson for us to learn is that God is never about the gift or the blessing. God is always about the relationship. Those with a healthy view of God understand that what is most important to God—and should be most important to us—is the relationship.

The amount of money the servants were given is irrelevant. What was important was that the master trusted them with his personal property. The first two servants understood that trust and the master's desire for relationship. Because they had a healthy view of him, they were able to draw close to their master.

The challenge today for those pursuing a relationship with God is that many modern Christian traditions underemphasize having a relationship with God. Emotionally distant and spiritually detached sermons that talk about the structure of the church and the duty of the Christian do little to inspire those seeking him.

Unless the pursuit of God is the first priority, people will be frustrated. If unhealthy assumptions and misconceptions about God are not corrected, the number of Christians both in this country and in the world will continue its downward spiral. Equally disturbing will be the number of people sitting in churches who will never experience the satisfaction and inspiration God intends them to have.

## AN UNHEALTHY VIEW OF GOD

> Then the man who had received one bag of gold came. "Master," he said, "I knew that you are a hard man, harvesting where you have not sown and gathering where you have not scattered seed. So I was afraid and went out and hid your gold in the ground. See, here is what belongs to you."
>
> Matthew 25:24–25

The first step for anyone seeking a powerful relationship with God is to examine and then dismantle any unhealthy views they have of him. The man who received one bag of gold gives us an example of how this unhealthiness might appear.

The one-bag man believed that he had a hard and unreasonable master. As a result, this man was afraid. He didn't trust his master. He didn't think his master was fair. He wasn't motivated to do anything for him. It wasn't a positive relationship.

When we approach God, the Bible, or prayer with negative assumptions about who God is or what he might do, we have an unhealthy view. This view of God will eventually become distant, de-motivating, and even destructive.

Our relationship with God has become distant if we consider him to be hard, and we won't want to share our feelings and emotions with him. Our relationship with God has become de-motivating when we no longer have a desire to know God, read the Bible, or even say a single prayer. The relationship has become destructive when our view of God negatively affects how he is seen by our spouse, children, and others whom we love. As a result, they may decide not to pursue a relationship with God.

These are just a few of the reasons why we need to aggressively address and change unhealthy attitudes about God. The questions we need to ask ourselves are as follows:

- Do I have a healthy or unhealthy view of God?
- What do my responses or reactions to God, the Bible, or prayer tell me about my view of God?
- How does my view of God affect my marriage, family, and relationships?

- How does my view of God affect my attitude toward Christians, attending church, or even making the decision to become a Christian?

## TURNING UNHEALTHY THOUGHTS INTO HEALTHY ONES

What comes into our minds when we think about God is the most important thing about us.

—A.W. Tozer[4]

When God is unattractive, it is usually a result of our having unhealthy rather than healthy thoughts about him. Here are some simple comparisons we can use to examine our own thoughts with regard to God.

### Turning Unhealthy Thoughts into Healthy Ones

| Unhealthy Thoughts | The Truth About God | Healthy Thoughts |
|---|---|---|
| He hurts me. | He cares for me. | He helps me feel. |
| He accuses me. | He understands me. | He softens my heart. |
| He limits me. | He believes in me. | He gives me a purpose. |
| He wants a performance. | He loves me. | He wants a relationship. |

## 1. HE CARES FOR ME

### MOVING FROM "HE HURTS ME" TO "HE HELPS ME FEEL"

> Look and see, there is no one at my right hand; no one is concerned for me. I have no refuge; no one cares for my life.
>
> Psalm 142:4

**Scan to listen to a music playlist on this topic.**

Of the many false statements that have been made about God, the worst are those that lead people to believe he doesn't care. On occasion, well-meaning religious people, including myself, have underestimated the importance of helping others to understand that God's central motivation is love. Everything God does is ultimately a result of the fact that he cares for us.

Many popular philosophers are eager to diminish God and very eager to diminish religion. They falsely lead people to believe that God is a clinical "it" rather than an emotional "he." They speak of God as though he has no heart or soul, which leads people to believe he is incapable of love or care. The result of these misrepresentations is that it has become far too easy for people to believe that God would rather hurt than help. This is simply not true. The majority of pain in life is simply the result of time and chance.

> I have seen something else under the sun: The race is not to the swift or the battle to the strong, nor does food come to the wise or wealth to the brilliant or favor to the learned; but time and chance happen to them all. Moreover, no one knows when their hour will come:

> As fish are caught in a cruel net, or birds are taken in a snare, so people are trapped by evil times that fall unexpectedly upon them.
>
> Ecclesiastes 9:11–12

If any spiritual force could be said to hurt us, it would be the spiritual force of darkness, the same one that was responsible for the pain in Job's life.

> "Does Job fear God for nothing?" Satan replied. "Have you not put a hedge around him and his household and everything he has? You have blessed the work of his hands, so that his flocks and herds are spread throughout the land. But now stretch out your hand and strike everything he has, and he will surely curse you to your face." The Lord said to Satan, "Very well, then, everything he has is in <u>your power</u>, but on the man himself do not lay a finger." Then Satan went out from the presence of the Lord.
>
> Job 1:9–12

Striking Job's life with pain was Satan's idea, not God's. It was Satan that caused negative things to happen to Job. Nevertheless, people said the pain was from God:

> ...another messenger came and said, "<u>The fire of God</u> fell from the heavens and burned up the sheep and the servants, and I am the only one who has escaped to tell you!"
>
> Job 1:16

God cares for us. He doesn't seek to hurt us. But at the same time he does not exempt us from Satan's attacks or the natural events of life. What he does is help us so that we don't harden ourselves to the pain. This would turn off our hearts. He helps us feel rather than let us harden. Feeling is essential if we are to experience life at its fullest.

> So I tell you this, and insist on it in the Lord, that you must no longer live as the Gentiles do, in the futility of their thinking. They are darkened in their understanding and separated from the life of God because of the ignorance that is in them due to the <u>hardening of their hearts</u>. Having lost all sensitivity, they have given themselves over to sensuality so as to indulge in every kind of impurity, and they are full of greed.
>
> Ephesians 4:17–19

Without God, we tend to harden ourselves to the pain in our lives. If we are overwhelmed by disappointment, loss, or regret, we can grow distant from those we love as well as from God.

Too often anger—along with resentment and bitterness—takes over. Before long we become hardened, and this hardness usually leads us to living life all alone.

> Again I saw something meaningless under the sun: <u>There was a man all alone</u>; he had neither son nor brother. There was no end to his toil, yet his eyes were not content with his wealth. "For whom am I toiling," he asked, "and why am I depriving myself of enjoyment?" This too is meaningless—a miserable business!
>
> Ecclesiastes 4:7–8

This is not God's plan for our lives. God cares.

> The LORD is good, a refuge in times of trouble. He cares for those who trust in him.
>
> Nahum 1:7

> Cast all your anxiety on him <u>because he cares for you</u>.
>
> 1 Peter 5:7

When we are in pain, when we are hurting and feeling alone, we need to banish the unhealthy thought that God has hurt us. Instead, we need to embrace the healthy thought that he has helped us to feel. Even during the most difficult and painful adversity and suffering, the ability to feel is what ultimately prevents the destruction of hope, health, and relationships. A heart that remains soft and aware of its need for God attracts his power. It is this power which allows us to both endure and overcome even the most overwhelming odds.

> Therefore, in order to keep me from becoming conceited, I was given a thorn in my flesh, a messenger of Satan, to torment me. Three times I pleaded with the Lord to take it away from me. But he said to me, "My grace is sufficient for you, for my power is made perfect in weakness." Therefore I will boast all the more gladly about my weaknesses, so that Christ's power may rest on me.
>
> 2 Corinthians 12:7–9

The goal is not merely to experience suffering but, with God's help, to fight and overcome it. This spirit to fight only exists in the hearts of those who know and trust they have a God on their side who cares for them.

## 2. HE UNDERSTANDS ME
### MOVING FROM "HE ACCUSES ME" TO "HE SOFTENS MY HEART"

> I will sprinkle clean water on you, and you will be clean; I will cleanse you from all your impurities and from all your idols. I will give you a new heart and put a new spirit in you; I will remove from you your heart of stone and give you a heart of flesh. And I will put my Spirit in you and move you to follow my decrees and be careful to keep my laws.
>
> Ezekiel 36:25–27

Many first-time Bible readers have a tendency to believe that God is preoccupied with making them feel guilty. Even a number of us who are experienced Bible readers can sometimes react in this way. We may feel accused of doing something wrong or committing yet another sin.

God is not nearly as focused on our record of wrongdoing as he is on the condition of our hearts. When it comes to sin, we might say that in God's eyes, "awareness is health." Those who see their sins and seek his help end up with a soft heart and a changed life. Not only can God forgive, but he can make us new.

> After removing Saul, he made David their king. God testified concerning him: "I have found David son of Jesse, a man after my own heart; he will do everything I want him to do."
>
> Acts 13:22

What made David such a significant figure in the Bible was that he understood that God wanted a relationship, not a performance. David knew that God was not as preoccupied with the sins he had committed as he was with how those sins had affected the relationship between the two of them.

This "relationship effect" is an especially important point to consider when teaching our children about God. We should not diminish the seriousness or importance of dealing with the sin in our lives, but we should emphasize the correct goal. God is looking for a soft heart, not a perfect life. He is looking for a relationship connection, not a stage performance.

God values our heart condition over our performance or behavior because he understands that what the heart loves and longs for, the heart will eventually do. In short, God understands us better than we can imagine.

> Do you not know? Have you not heard? The LORD is the everlasting God, the Creator of the ends of the earth. He will not grow tired or weary, and his understanding no one can fathom.
>
> Isaiah 40:28

The next time we fail to live up to the rules and feel accused or overwhelmed with guilt, we must remember that God understands. He understands our discouragement and defeat, our regret and loss. He knows our feelings of loneliness and embarrassment and the burning desire to run from responsibility. He understands that we may be feeling completely alone.

We should not run from him in fear, but run to him in relief and with a soft heart. That is what he has wanted all along—regardless of what Christian religious tradition may have taught us and regardless of what our desire to perform may be tempting us to do.

## 3. HE BELIEVES IN ME
## MOVING FROM "HE LIMITS ME" TO "HE GIVES ME PURPOSE"

> "About noon, King Agrippa, as I was on the road, I saw a light from heaven, brighter than the sun, blazing around me and my companions. We all fell to the ground, and I heard a voice saying to me in Aramaic, 'Saul, Saul, why do you persecute me? <u>It is hard for you to kick against the goads.</u>'"
>
> Acts 26:13–14

After I decided to make God the top priority in my life and became a Christian, I began to feel limited. It seemed like everything I wanted to do was either a sin or a bad spiritual decision. I felt trapped and began to question my decision to live the Christian life.

Around that time, I heard a sermon based on Revelation 3:14–16. The speaker explained that those who follow God fall into one of three categories: hot, cold, or lukewarm. Those who are considered lukewarm are on the fence. They won't fully commit to God or the world. These lukewarm people are the ones who hurt God the most.

That's when I realized that God wasn't limiting me, but that my love for him was lukewarm. Like Paul who kicked against the goads, I was kicking against God's Word. It was only when I recognized that I was fighting God—not being limited by him—that I was able to open my eyes and see. Rather than limiting me, God was leading me to my destiny. He was trying to show me his purpose for my life.

Since then, I have recognized that when I feel frustrated and limited, I need to stop and ask the question, "Where is God trying to lead me?" The truth is that God does not limit me. Instead, he deeply believes in me.

## 4. HE LOVES ME

## MOVING FROM "HE WANTS A PERFORMANCE" TO "HE WANTS A RELATIONSHIP"

> The Lord says: "These people <u>come near to me with their mouth</u> and <u>honor me with their lips</u>, but <u>their hearts are far from me</u>. Their worship of me is based on merely human rules they have been taught."
>
> Isaiah 29:13

Of all the unhealthy thoughts we can have, one of the most difficult ones to change is that God wants a performance rather than a relationship. The reason for this difficulty is that providing God with a performance merely requires a change of behavior. On the other hand, building a relationship with God requires a change of heart. Unfortunately, since we find it easier to change our behavior than the condition of our hearts, we choose to perform for God rather than seek a relationship with him. The problem with this type of thinking is that it underestimates the love and power of God.

> I will give you a new heart and put a new spirit in you; I will remove from you your heart of stone and give you a heart of flesh. And I will put my Spirit in you and move you to follow my decrees and be careful to keep my laws.
>
> Ezekiel 36:26–27

God loves us enough to change us. We simply need to focus on building a relationship with him rather than performing. How do we do this?

The first step is deciding to seek a relationship with God rather than trying to be successful at Christianity. This leads to the next step, which is deriving our security from our intimacy with God rather than our sinless record. When we are most motivated by our desire for God and the degree of closeness in that relationship, we put aside the pursuit of perfection in favor of his unconditional love. This type of relationship-based thinking is contrasted with performance-based thinking in the chart on the next page.

Examine the columns to determine where your strengths and weaknesses lie, so you can ask God to change your heart inclinations. Take a look at the different questions, so you can better understand how to move from performance-based to relationship-based thinking.

Always remember that a performance-based relationship with God is dangerous because we will never understand or experience his unconditional love. We will never know the freedom of admitting our sins, experiencing forgiveness, and having the burden of guilt lifted from our consciences. In the end, we won't even enjoy Christianity because we will never feel that being ourselves is good enough. Performance-based Christians can never relax and will eventually burn out on God, church, and Christianity.

Relationship-based Christians experience something completely different. The great advantage they enjoy is the certainty that God really loves them. Having invested in seeking, knowing, and understanding God's heart, they know that a relationship is his great desire.

It is this desire for a relationship that drives God to care for, understand, and believe in us. He wants our heart, not our performance. Relationship-based Christians give God their heart. They understand that while we must take sin seriously, we must also remember that sin does not define who we are to God.

### Moving from Performance-Focused to Relationship-Focused
Make note of your strengths and weaknesses.

| Performance-Focused | Relationship-Focused | The Difference |
|---|---|---|
| Seek success. | Seek God. | Are you more motivated by God or success? |
| Prefer sinless record. | Desire intimacy. | Does relationship intimacy or a sinless record make you feel most secure? |
| Behavior change. | Heart change. | Do you work on changing your heart or settle for changing your behavior? |
| Motivated by rewards. | Motivated by relationships. | What motivates you and how do you motivate others? |
| Failure is fatal. | Resilent in failure. | How well and how quickly do you recover from failure? |
| Hide sin. | Admit sin. | Do you see the admission of sin as bringing you closer to or driving you farther away from God and people? |
| Hide shame and guilt. | Seek forgiveness. | Do you seek forgiveness or seek to prove your innocence? |
| Fearful and insecure. | Confident and secure. | Do you feel unconditionally liked and loved by God and people? |

Who we are to God is defined by the relationship our hearts have with his heart. What does this mean? It means we need to have loving answers to these questions:

- Do I like God?
- Do I want to be close to him?
- Do I think about God throughout the day?
- Would I be satisfied if he never gave me another blessing beyond this relationship?
- Do I look forward to spending time with him?
- Am I aware of and desirous of his presence and influence in my life?
- Is he as real to me as any human relationship?
- Can I relax with him, trust him, and enjoy him?

Until we can answer these questions positively and change our unhealthy thoughts to healthy ones, it will be difficult for us to find God attractive. Can it be done? Can we change our thoughts and feelings about God? Absolutely! People in the Bible did it all the time. We can transform our relationship with God if we, like them, will invest the time, effort, and energy. God can and will become more attractive to us.

In our next chapter, we will tackle a subject that has made God unattractive to far too many people: religion. We will learn how religion can replace God, and why that can cause people to find him unattractive. We will also learn what we can do to practice our faith in a way that restores God's attractiveness.

**HE'S NOT WHO YOU THINK HE IS**

## DIVE DEEP: Pause and Reflect
Jot down notes you want to remember from each section

*Turning Unhealthy Thoughts into Healthy Ones*

**1.1 WHEN GOD ISN'T ATTRACTIVE**
Matthew 6:24, Matthew 25:14-18
What are your thoughts and feelings now about God?

**1.2 A HEALTHY VIEW OF GOD**
Matthew 25:19-23

**1.3 AN UNHEALTHY VIEW OF GOD**
Matthew 25:24-25

**1.4 TURNING UNHEALTHY THOUGHTS INTO HEALTHY ONES**
1. He cares for me: Turning "He hurts me" into "He helps me feel"
Matthew 25:24-25, Psalm 142:4, Ecclesiastes 9:11-12, Job 1:9-11, Job 1:16, Ephesians 4:17-19, Ecclesiastes 4:7-8, Nahum 1:7, 1 Peter 5:7, 2 Corinthians 12:7-9

**1.4 TURNING UNHEALTHY THOUGHTS INTO HEALTHY ONES (CONTINUED...)**
2. He understands me: Turning "He accuses me" into "He softens my heart"
Ezekiel 36:25-27, Acts 13:22, Isaiah 40:28

3. He believes in me: Turning "He limits me" into "He gives me purpose"
Acts 26:13-14
Where is God trying to lead me?

4. He loves me: Turning "He wants a performance" into "He wants a relationship"
Isaiah 29:13, Ezekiel 36:26-27
Do I like God? Do I want to be close to him? Can I relax with him, trust him, and enjoy him?

**1 BIG TAKEAWAY:**

Scan this QR code with your phone's camera to check out the latest resources on this chapter here

## CHAPTER TWO:
# WHEN RELIGION BECOMES GOD

*Understanding the Difference Between God and Religion*

"Are you tired? Worn out? Burned out on religion? Come to me. Get away with me and you'll recover your life. I'll show you how to take a real rest. Walk with me and work with me—watch how I do it. Learn the unforced rhythms of grace. I won't lay anything heavy or ill-fitting on you. Keep company with me and you'll learn to live freely and lightly."

Matthew 11:28–30, The Message

I loved the college dorm life, and one of the best aspects of that experience was the late-night talks. I can remember one evening in particular when someone posed the question, "Does anyone here believe in God?"

My first thought was not about God. My first thought was about myself. The answer that I gave would influence other people's opinions of me. I wanted to be known as one cool customer—intelligent and likeable. Searching through my memory banks, I fashioned an answer appropriate for my desired outcome. I said, "I am agnostic, and I can't stand organized religion."

In my view it was the perfect answer. As an agnostic, I wasn't saying yes or no to the existence of God. I wouldn't lose any friends and no one would be offended—that made me likeable. By saying I disliked organized religion, I was part of a popular and growing trend—one that gave people a politically correct way to bow out of religion. That was cool! Overall, my answer reflected an attitude that was not only acceptable but favorable with the intelligentsia of the academic world. It would score big points on the smart meter. Mission accomplished!

What I didn't admit to myself at that time was that nothing I said expressed the truth of how I really felt about God. The truth was that I believed in God, but I didn't believe in religion. I saw God as genuine, caring, and capable of helping in even the most difficult circumstances. I liked him. At the same time I felt that religious people fell into one of three categories—self-righteous, hypocritical, or very average. It wasn't that I disliked religious people as much as I preferred the company of those who were more normal or successful.

That dorm room discussion took place in 1979. My negative feelings almost kept me from giving God a chance and almost cost me my relationship with God. Those negative feelings are surprisingly similar to what many people today feel toward religious people and religious organizations.

What I didn't understand then, but I realize now, is that I didn't disbelieve God—I disliked religion. I had allowed my observations of and experiences with religion to color my view of God. I had allowed religion to become synonymous with

God. I didn't see God; I saw church. I didn't see God; I saw clergy. I didn't see God; I saw the religious right. I didn't see God; I saw only Christians whom I could criticize and diminish because of their weaknesses and sins.

I burned out on religion before I ever seriously pursued a relationship with God. That is exactly what happens today to many people who find God unattractive. They think it is God they are rejecting when, in reality, it is religion. They are repulsed by religion because religion was never meant to be our god.

## HOW RELIGION BECOMES GOD

> If you're brought up Jewish, don't assume that you can lean back in the arms of your religion and take it easy, feeling smug because you're an insider to God's revelation, a connoisseur of the best things of God, informed on the latest doctrines! I have a special word of caution for you who are sure that you have it all together yourselves and, because you know God's revealed Word inside and out, feel qualified to guide others through their blind alleys and dark nights and confused emotions to God.
>
> Romans 2:17-20, The Message

God is attractive. His love, care, and concern for us make him appealing. His belief in us makes him desirable. His expectation for us is inspiring. His willingness to forgive, forget, and give us a second chance makes him irresistible. Those who truly know God practice a religion that reflects these qualities. For those who know him, God remains at all times at the forefront of their lives. In their minds, he is the most attractive thing about their faith.

Unfortunately, as attractive as God may be, we have been known to forget him. We become preoccupied with the success he has given us and the amazing things he has done through us. Before we know it, we are talking about how great we are rather than how great he is—and religion is born. Too often when religion is birthed, the created becomes more important than the Creator.

> They exchanged the truth about God for a lie, and worshiped and served created things rather than the Creator—who is forever praised. Amen.
>
> Romans 1:25

Religion is defined by the Merriam-Webster Dictionary as "a personal set or institutionalized system of religious attitudes, beliefs, and practices."[5] This definition explains exactly what happens when religion displaces God. Things become more individual and institutionalized. God, and especially his Word, become less relevant than our personal point of view or the view of the institution to which we belong.

When religion becomes God, we become more important than he is. Suddenly, what matters most is the name, style, and reputation of our church. We begin the unspiritual pursuit of position, the unhealthy quest for attention, and engage in ugly internecine battles for influence. These competitive attitudes soon produce chronic disagreement and division.

These dramas play out in full view of those who have not yet made up their minds about religion or God. When a group of believers lose their focus on God, onlookers may see their actions as a reflection of who God is and what he is like. As a result, those people who are watching never come to know God.

## WHY THIS MATTERS

> For fools speak folly, their hearts are bent on evil: They practice ungodliness and spread error concerning the Lord; the hungry they leave empty and from the thirsty they withhold water.
>
> Isaiah 32:6

In my view, the single greatest reason for the ever-increasing number of people who are selecting "none" when asked about their religious beliefs is that religion is becoming god. The loud, conflicting, and confusing presence of religion is making it more and more difficult for people to see who God really is.

> *In Pew Research Center telephone surveys conducted in 2018 and 2019, 65% of American adults describe themselves as Christians when asked about their religion, down 12 percentage points over the past decade. Meanwhile, the religiously unaffiliated share of the population, consisting of people who describe their religious identity as atheist, agnostic or "nothing in particular," now stands at 26%, up from 17% in 2009.*
>
> *The changes underway in the American religious landscape are broad-based. The Christian share of the population is down and religious "nones" have grown across multiple demographic groups: white people, black people and Hispanics; men and women; in all regions of the country;*

> *and among college graduates and those with lower levels of educational attainment. Religious "nones" are growing faster among Democrats than Republicans, though their ranks are swelling in both partisan coalitions. And although the religiously unaffiliated are on the rise among younger people and most groups of older adults, their growth is most pronounced among young adults.*[6]

Why does any of this matter? Religion is making God unattractive, and what seems like a distant statistic today may eventually find its way into our own living rooms.

## CHANGE OR LOSE OUR CHILDREN

> The mildest criticism of religion is also the most radical and the most devastating one. Religion is man-made. Even the men who made it cannot agree on what their prophets or redeemers or gurus actually said or did.
>
> – Christoper Hitchens[7]

Christopher Hitchens' controversial book has met with no small amount of resistance from the religious establishment, but I believe his fundamental premise deserves reflection. He first says, "God Is Not Great." Then, as if to prove his point, he goes on to say, "Religion Poisons Everything."

Hitchens' reasons for not liking religion are many, and they are well argued. But by his own admission "religion is man-made," so what does he expect? What Hitchens sees is that when man places himself at the center of religion, religion will poison. That is exactly what has been happening with too many of us today.

When we allow ourselves to live and to lead without keeping God at the center of our lives, the greatest casualties will be our young people. Already, they are seeing too much religion and too little God. This is dangerous and requires urgent correction because trends show that future generations will be staying away from religion in general, and from churches, specifically.

> *Most young adults today don't pray, don't worship and don't read the Bible, a major survey by a Christian research firm shows. If the trends continue, "the millennial generation will see churches closing as quickly as GM dealerships," says Thom Rainer, president of LifeWay Christian Resources. In the group's survey of 1,200, 18- to 29-year-olds, 72% say they're "really more spiritual than religious."[8]*

In this same survey, sixty-eight percent of young adults did not consider anything closely related to religion to be among the most important things in their life. Thirty-six percent rarely, if ever, read the Bible, while fifty percent attended church less than once a week.

The failure to restore God to his rightful place will cost us our children. It will also cost us the chance to inspire family, friends, and neighbors to know and understand our great God. In the end, it is also likely to cost us our own relationship with God. In our disillusionment, what we will see as a failure on God's part will be, in reality, a failure of man-made religion.

## WHAT DOES CHANGE LOOK LIKE

> For I tell you that unless your righteousness surpasses that of the Pharisees and the teachers of the law, you will certainly not enter the kingdom of heaven.
>
> Matthew 5:20

Religion doesn't have to become god. People don't have to be turned off to religion and churches don't have to descend into a torrent of infighting and division. God can make religion inspiring for the experienced as well as for the young believer. All we have to do is accept and embrace change.

Keeping God as our central focus should not be considered a one-time project or campaign, but our life's work. We should embrace a life of continual growth and change—one that leads to ongoing progress in our walk with God. It is this mindset alone that will keep religion from becoming god.

Fortunately for us, Jesus gave us a simple blueprint for change: don't be a Pharisee! In Jesus' day, the Pharisees were known as experts in Scriptural law. Their practice of Jewish religion involved following strict traditions that weren't necessarily in the Scriptures. And all too often, the Pharisees' religion became their god—much to the spiritual detriment of themselves and those around them (read Matthew 23 for a more in-depth look at what Jesus had to say about Pharisees).

There are four things we can do in our personal lives as well as in our churches that will keep religion from becoming god. They are all rooted in the conviction that we must never become like the Pharisees.

## 1. MAKE THE BIBLE OUR STANDARD

> Then some Pharisees and teachers of the law came to Jesus from Jerusalem and asked, "Why do your disciples break the tradition of the elders? They don't wash their hands before they eat!" Jesus replied, "And why do you break the command of God for the sake of your tradition?"
>
> Matthew 15:1–3

When human opinion and tradition become more important than the Bible, we are well on our way to making a god of our religion. Therefore, it is of vital importance that we make the Bible the ultimate standard in our lives and churches.

## 2. EMPHASIZE CLOSENESS TO GOD

> You hypocrites! Isaiah was right when he prophesied about you: "These people honor me with their lips, but their hearts are far from me. They worship me in vain; their teachings are merely human rules."
>
> Matthew 15:7-9

God's grievance with the Pharisees was that they were not close to him. Although they did their duty, there was no love—no passion or excitement—in their relationship with him. Feeling distant, detached, and unmoved by our relationship with God should serve as a warning sign that our faith is becoming a religion—something we do rather than something we believe. When we reach this point, we need to examine our hearts to discover what might be creating spiritual distance from God. Then we need to shift our focus to restoring intimacy in our relationship with him.

## 3. LOVE GOD, NOT ATTENTION

> Then Jesus said to the crowds and to his disciples: "The teachers of the law and the Pharisees sit in Moses' seat. So you must be careful to do everything they tell you. But do not do what they do, for they do not practice what they preach. They tie up heavy, cumbersome loads and put them on other people's shoulders, but they themselves are not willing to lift a finger to move them.

> "Everything they do is done for people to see: They make their phylacteries wide and the tassels on their garments long; they love the place of honor at banquets and the most important seats in the synagogues; they love to be greeted with respect in the marketplaces and to be called 'Rabbi' by others."
>
> Matthew 23:1–7

One of the simplest and quickest routes to making a god of religion is to love attention more than God. This may well have been the core problem experienced by the Pharisees in their relationship with him.

Jesus makes a scathing observation about them when he says, "Everything they do is done for men to see." Then he talks about specifics and lists all the things they love, and each one of them is a way to get attention.

Religion becomes god when we are consumed by appearances and we focus our efforts on getting attention or gaining position. In contrast, we treat God as God if we are satisfied with him and what he gives us.

## 4. BUILD INSIDE-OUT RELATIONSHIPS

> "Woe to you, teachers of the law and Pharisees, you hypocrites! You clean the outside of the cup and dish, but inside they are full of greed and self-indulgence. Blind Pharisee! First clean the inside of the cup and dish, and then the outside also will be clean."
>
> Matthew 23:25–26

The Pharisees built superficial relationships. Their focus was on appearances. As long as they looked good, everything was good. These are the kinds of relationships that will cause religion to be dominant and God to be diminished.

When our focus is solely on outward appearances, we will never realize how much we need God. It is only when we look inside and grapple with the reality of our lives that our need for God becomes apparent. Deep relationships are built from the inside out and are essential if we are to keep religion from becoming god for us.

In our next chapter we will see that—as tempting as it might be to replace God with religion—an even greater danger is that we will replace him with people. We will learn how to overcome this temptation, keep our focus on God, and build healthy relationships with people.

Take a look at this chart to identify how our focus changes when religion becomes God:

## 4 Ways That People and Churches Change When Religion Becomes God

**The focus shifts from "God" to "people."**
- The question shifts from "What does the Bible say?" to "What do I say?"
- The question shifts from "What does God want?" to "What do I want?"

**The focus shifts from "relationships" to "memberships."**
- The question shifts from "How do I love people?" to "What do I need to do?"
- The question shifts from "Can we get together?" to "Do I have to attend?"

**The focus shifts from "God's purpose" to "my position."**
- The question shifts from "How can I help people?" to "What role do I play?"
- The question shifts from "What more can we do?" to "Why are we doing that?"

**The focus shifts from "being spiritual" to "being worldly."**
- The question shifts from "How am I doing?" to "How do I look?"
- The question shifts from "Will you help me?" to "Why don't you leave me alone?"

**CHAPTER TWO: WHEN RELIGION BECOMES GOD**

## DIVE DEEP: Pause and Reflect
Jot down notes you want to remember from each section

**2.1 HOW RELIGION BECOMES GOD**
Matthew 11:28-30, Romans 2:17-20, Romans 1:25

**2.2 WHY THIS MATTERS**
Isaiah 32:6

**2.3 CHANGE OR LOSE OUR CHILDREN**

**2.4 WHAT DOES CHANGE LOOK LIKE?**
Matthew 5:20

1. Make the Bible our standard
Matthew 15:1-3

2. Emphasize closeness to God
Matthew 15:7-9

3. Love God not attention
Matthew 23:1-7

4. Build inside out relationships
Matthew 23:25-26

Understanding the Difference Between God and Religion

**BIG TAKEAWAY:**

Scan this QR code with your phone's camera to check out the latest resources on this chapter here

# CHAPTER THREE:
# WHEN PEOPLE BECOME GOD

*Overcoming the Fear of Being Different*

> But my servant Caleb—<u>this is a different story</u>. He has <u>a different spirit</u>; he follows me <u>passionately</u>. I'll bring him into the land that he scouted and his children will inherit it.
>
> Numbers 14:24, The Message

In the previous chapter, we talked about the human tendency to replace God with religion and what we can do to overcome it. An even more common tendency is to replace God with people. When we cling to people rather than to God, we forfeit the destiny to which God has called us and settle for what people want us to be.

> Those who cling to worthless idols turn away from God's love for them.
>
> Jonah 2:8

When people become god, we acquiesce to the pressure of popular opinion and silence the dream that God has placed within us. Under the condescending glare of the crowd, we choose to conform rather than to make a difference. In the end, these human forces instill in us a deep and paralyzing fear of being different, smothering the transformative power God has given each one of us to become who we were meant to be.

> Do not conform to the pattern of this world, but be transformed by the renewing of your mind. Then you will be able to test and approve what God's will is—his good, pleasing and perfect will.
>
> Romans 12:2

As long as we conform to the pattern of this world, we won't be able to develop a transformational relationship with God. We won't be able to see the destiny he has in mind for us, nor will we be able to make this dream come true.

Those who devote themselves to developing a great relationship with God are not merely seeking the doctrinal plan of salvation or his comfort in times of pain and difficulty. A relationship with God is also about rising above the apathy, lethargy, and mediocrity that motivate people to conform and settle. It is about being changed and transformed; it is about overcoming the fear of being different.

Those who seek to know God in this way are following in the footsteps of Caleb, a man who stood with God at the risk of being different. As a result, Caleb played a significant role in inspiring and leading the Israelites to conquer the promised land, and to help them fulfill the destiny to which God had called them.

God has provided a destiny for each one of us, just as he did for Caleb. It is a destiny as specific and personal as the one he communicated to the prophet Jeremiah.

> The word of the Lord came to me, saying, "<u>Before I formed you in the womb</u> I knew you, <u>before you were born</u> I set you apart; I appointed you as a prophet to the nations."
>
> Jeremiah 1:4–5

Psalm 139 tells us that the story of our destiny has been written in God's book. If we choose to walk with him in this life, those pages will begin to be fulfilled. We will start living a life that will inspire others.

> My frame was not hidden from you when I was made in the secret place, when I was woven together in the depths of the earth. Your eyes saw my unformed body; all the days ordained for me were <u>written in your book</u> before one of them came to be.
>
> Psalm 139:15–16

This life of inspiration is one in which we will never walk alone. He will first help us discover what it means to seek, find, and know him better. As we learn to walk intimately with him on the journey of our lives, we will discover and fulfill the destiny to which he has called us. We will come to know the God who loves us and is deeply involved in the intimate details of our lives.

> From one man he made all the nations, that they should inhabit the whole earth; and <u>he marked out their appointed times in history</u> and the boundaries of their lands. God did this so that they would seek him and perhaps reach out for him and find him, though he is not far from any one of us.
>
> Acts 17:26–27

The only thing that stands in the way of these promises becoming our reality is our fear of being different. I believe God works throughout our lives to help us overcome this fear. Once we overcome it, we are no longer susceptible to making people our god. Free to see God without human interference, we will be able to discover his true attraction and our ultimate destiny.

## IT'S OKAY TO BE DIFFERENT

> If a man does not keep pace with his companions, perhaps it is because he hears a different drummer. Let him <u>step to the music which he hears</u>, however measured or far away.
>
> —Henry David Thoreau[9]

Looking back on my life, as well as the lives of many of my closest friends, I can see that God was at work from the very beginning. From our earliest days he was reaching out, guiding, and teaching us, in the hope that we would choose him. I think he was hoping we wouldn't be afraid to be different. I am sure if you examine your life, you will feel the same way.

I was not raised to be religious. I was raised to trust and respect God. I was also raised to be different—not to feel that I had to conform or comply, but that I could think and act for myself, regardless of how others might respond. Although they did not do it purposely, my parents could not have found a better way to point me to God. They could not have found a better way to prepare me to fulfill my destiny.

I was born in Wichita, Kansas. I lived with my mom, dad, and two older sisters in an apartment complex that I remember with great fondness. I remember playing games of baseball, kickball, and football with the neighborhood kids. I remember the entire community disappearing from sight as everyone entered their homes to watch the Wizard of Oz on television. I also remember talking to the policeman stationed outside our complex, because the local government feared that the rioting occurring in Black neighborhoods across the country would come to Wichita.

I attended Head Start and kindergarten at Little School and, just like in my apartment complex, everyone was Black. By the time I was ready to enter second grade, my parents had improved their financial position and moved us to an affluent and predominantly white community in the suburbs of Wichita.

This was 1968 and although the world around me was shaking, I had been largely unaffected by the controversial and explosive social issues of the day. That all changed when I attended my new school.

I was seven years old and entering second grade. When I arrived in class, I quickly realized that I was different. I was the only Black child in a classroom of about twenty-five students, and if my memory serves me correctly, it was my first experience with a white teacher. She was very old.

Everything seemed normal until the day came to write our names on our math books. We first wrote our names on a separate piece of paper, and then the teacher came by to check our spelling. When she came to me, she insisted that I had misspelled my last name.

I told her that I had spelled it correctly. I said, "My last name is "Ewell" (pronounced like the word "Yule") and is spelled "E-w-e-l-l." She disagreed and made me write my name on my math book as "Elwell" (pronounced in two syllables as "El-well"). So I took the permanent black marker, and spelled out "E-L-W-E-L-L."

I didn't want to write those letters on my book, but fear made me change my name. The fear of creating a scene, of getting in trouble, and of making it even more obvious to everyone that I was "different."

When I returned home from school, my mom heard what had happened. She then visited the school and apparently introduced that teacher to the twentieth century. Afterward I received a new math book with my name spelled correctly.

I learned three things from my mother's response:

1. Never be ashamed of who you are.
2. Never be intimidated by people.
3. Educate the unenlightened.

In a nutshell, on this one day I learned a transformational lesson: It's okay to be different.

My mom taught it, but I am certain God was behind it, which leads to a question: Can we look at our lives and discover the moments when God was trying to draw us close to him by teaching us this same lesson—that "It's okay to be different"?

## THINK DIFFERENTLY

> As Paul talked about righteousness, self-control and the judgment to come, Felix was afraid and said, "That's enough for now! You may leave. <u>When I find it convenient</u>, I will send for you."
>
> Acts 24:25

Developing and building a relationship with God will never be convenient. It will always require that we make changes, that we become different. It is perhaps the original "Inconvenient Truth." When we accept the truth that it's okay to be different, we will find the decision to pursue God much easier.

When we live a God-centered rather than a people-centered life, we will have to think differently. The difference is not in merely reading the Bible, praying, or attending church. The difference is that we are deciding that people will not be our god. Nowhere is this type of thinking more needed than in the church.

Perhaps you have noticed the increasing number of people who are choosing to seek God without the help of a church. They are, in effect, saying that church makes God unattractive. What is the problem? Why do they feel that attending church gets in the way of knowing God?

The problem with church is that we are introduced first to the people who attend, so it is easy for them to become our central focus. Things might be better if we met God first, but it is usually the other way around. We focus on the speakers, singers, members, or any other human factor. We become so focused on people that we fail to hear or see God.

We end up choosing our church based on the race, style, socioeconomic status, and likability of the members. Whether or not we find these people attractive will determine how we feel about the church, and quite often how we feel about God.

The solution many people have found is to shun church altogether. This avoids the problem, but it doesn't solve it. We need to deal with the real problem. If we cannot belong to a church without having our relationships with people interfere with our pursuit of God, we need to learn how to think differently.

Thinking differently means focusing on God rather than focusing on people. This is what Samuel had to do when he mistakenly turned to Eli instead of turning to God.

> Then the LORD called Samuel. Samuel answered, "Here I am." And he ran to Eli and said, "Here I am; you called me." But Eli said, "I did not call; go back and lie down." So he went and lay down. Again the LORD called, "Samuel!" And Samuel got up and went to Eli and said, "Here I am; you called me." "My son," Eli said, "I did not call; go back and lie down." <u>Now Samuel did not yet know the LORD</u>: The word of the LORD had not yet been revealed to him. A third time the LORD called, "Samuel!" And Samuel got up and went to Eli and said, "Here I am; you called me." Then Eli realized that the LORD was calling the boy.
>
> 1 Samuel 3:4–8

I understand and relate to Samuel's confusion. When I was first invited to a Bible study group in college, I attended because the person who invited me was a very good basketball player. I needed good players for my college intramural team and thought that attending his Bible study would give me a better chance of successfully recruiting him for my team.

Until my friend convinced me to read and study the Bible for myself, his voice was all I heard. After some time, I decided to attend an actual church service. I can still remember this strange journey and how it felt. It was the same journey taken by many people who have long avoided or ignored church.

I felt like I had gone back in time. In a historic sense, the church building was pretty nice. The wooden benches reminded me of a time gone by, and, compared to the music I listened to on the radio, the songs seemed extremely dated. While the sermon was energetic, I couldn't understand much of it because I wasn't familiar with their Christian language.

As I looked around, I remember asking myself how I felt about these people and if I liked them. In my estimation, the church wasn't doing too well. By the time the lengthy service was over, I couldn't wait to get out of there.

The result was that I did what thousands of people like me have done for hundreds of years: I saw the people, I didn't see God. I wasn't attracted to the people that day, so I pretty much decided that church and its version of God were unattractive.

I continued my basketball recruitment efforts of my Christian friend, and with his encouragement, I continued reading the Bible. In time I began to see something I hadn't noticed before. I began to see God rather than the church; I began to see God rather than the people. It really made a difference in the way I looked at everything. It made me think differently.

I learned about the impact of sin, the sacrifice of Jesus on the cross, and the fact that God was in passionate pursuit of a relationship with me. This inspired me because, in my heart, I had always sensed there was a God. I had simply never known how to find him.

Once I found God, I saw the people and the church very differently. I saw the world around me very differently. I no longer took things at face value or felt confined by who I thought people wanted me to be. It was a little like the movie

*The Matrix* when Neo chooses the red pill and has his eyes opened. After that, it wasn't long until I decided I wanted a relationship with God and became a Christian.

## THINKING TRADITIONALLY

> Now the Lord is the Spirit, and where the Spirit of the Lord is, there is freedom.
>
> 2 Corinthians 3:17

Learning to live the Christian life and walk with God was extremely liberating. I was no longer afraid to be different. I felt free to be me. I was able to leave behind all the games I had played in the world.

We have all played those games. *How do I look? How do I measure up? What are people thinking and saying about me? Who loves me? Who cares about me? How will people react once they know me? Can I tell people what I really think?*

I felt free of all of this debilitating self-talk and many more things I don't have time to describe in these pages.

I entered the church with no religious background to speak of, so I didn't realize that churches, like societies, have their own cultures. Although we don't like to admit it, churches can have their own set of games to be played. These are called traditions, and while they have little or nothing to do with the Bible, they are held very dear by some in the church community.

I ran smack dab into these traditions when I decided I wanted to become a leader in the church. To be honest, the traditions were not all that bad and hardly need to be recalled in this space. Their danger was not in their content, but in their focus. They placed the focus back on people. Suddenly I was less worried about how I looked to God and more worried about how I looked to people. Through no one's fault but my own, I began to slowly, and almost imperceptibly, lose connection with God.

> <u>They have lost connection with the head</u>, from whom the whole body, supported and held together by its ligaments and sinews, <u>grows as God causes it to grow</u>.
>
> Colossians 2:19

I grew in my leadership ability as well as my effectiveness at helping people become Christians, but I was not growing in my personal relationship with God. I was volunteering, serving, and working in every way I could to advance up the ladder of spiritual "success." My focus on people was increasing while at the same time my interest in God was decreasing. I became more concerned with the rules of the church than I was with my relationship with God.

The same fear of being different that I had felt outside the church, I was now feeling inside the church, precisely because I had made the people in the church into my god.

> Since you died with Christ to the elemental spiritual forces of this world, why, as though you still belonged to the world, do you submit to its rules: "Do not handle! Do not taste! Do not touch!"? These rules, which have to do with things that are all destined to perish with use, are based on merely human commands and teachings. Such regulations indeed have an appearance of wisdom, with their self-imposed worship, their false humility and their harsh treatment of the body, but they lack any value in restraining sensual indulgence.
>
> Colossians 2:20–23

I began to crash spiritually. I was burning out. I began to pretend more and share my true spiritual condition less. Rather than being motivated by my relationship with God, I was energized by attention, selfish ambition, and the achievement of position. After escaping the rat race of the world, I had now turned the church into a rat race by abandoning God and worshiping people. I was losing the courage to be different.

## THE RIVER, THE TREE, AND MY FRIENDS

> Answer me, Lord, answer me, so these people will know that you, Lord, are God, and that you are turning their hearts back again.
>
> 1 Kings 18:37

I have experienced the spiritual burnout cycle I have just described on more than one occasion in my Christian life. Each time I could have blamed God or the church, but doing so would have only deepened my focus on people. To truly recover the gift of freedom God had offered me, I needed to return to him. Returning to him was the only way I could stop living for people, stop being afraid of being different, and rediscover what it meant to think differently. In short, I needed to experience a turning point.

Over the years I have learned that God is always guiding me toward these turning points so that he and I can enjoy an ever-increasing closeness. Three of these turning points in particular have helped me in some of my most difficult times, and I want to share them with you.

**HE'S NOT WHO YOU THINK HE IS**

CHAPTER THREE: WHEN PEOPLE BECOME GOD

## THE RIVER

> Then I came to the colony of Judean exiles in Tel-abib, beside the Kebar River. I was overwhelmed and sat among them for seven days.
>
> Ezekiel 3:15, NLT

The first turning point in my spiritual life came when I considered leaving God and the church. I didn't like how my life was going. On the one hand, I loved the person I had been before I came to church, and I missed him. I also loved who I had become with God and longed to be that person too. I felt torn between both worlds, and I was experiencing a crisis of faith. I was overwhelmed like Ezekiel, who sat by the Kebar River. Interestingly enough, I found my own river.

One spring night in my sophomore year of college, I walked out of my dorm room and took a walk that overlooked the Charles River in Boston, Massachusetts. I told God that I didn't much like where my life was at and that, in my mind, I needed to make a decision. Either I was going to remain in the church for the rest of my life, or I was going to leave now. It was a long walk.

There was no one on this walk with me—except God. I didn't consult with any family members or friends about this decision. As young as I was in the faith, I realized that God was my reason for being there. This was not a decision about membership in a human organization, but a question of how I would treat God. He—and he alone—would be most affected by my leaving the church.

I decided to stay. But that wasn't the most important thing that happened on that warm spring night in 1980. The most important thing was that, at a crucial turning point, I established a pattern of going to God for an answer, rather than to people. This lesson has served me well throughout my life. I encourage you to do the same.

## THE TREE

> Then he went on alone into the wilderness, traveling all day. He sat down under a solitary broom tree and prayed that he might die. "I have had enough, Lord," he said. "Take my life, for I am no better than my ancestors who have already died."
>
> 1 Kings 19:4, NLT

Something I have tried to learn from the turning points in my life is that when I feel like I have failed, I need to keep the drama to a minimum. I can remember the failures of my spiritual life quite vividly and when retelling the stories, my usual practice is to recall them with great drama.

Through the years, my wife and close spiritual friends have helped me to understand that I have often blown these stories up to be much more than they really were. This is not surprising, since I am a very emotional person. Perhaps you are like me. Perhaps you are like Elijah. Both of us ended up under a tree, feeling extremely defeated and highly emotional.

My time under the tree came after a series of big spiritual wins. Riding high on pride, I thought I had arrived. I became enamored of myself, my ability to lead, and my ability to attract attention. As one might imagine, my interest in God had declined. My energy was being fueled by how people felt about me. This felt so good that I was losing my desire for God.

It wasn't long before I crashed and burned spiritually. Suddenly I found myself sitting under a tree in the city of Cambridge, Massachusetts, contemplating spiritual failure. How had I gotten myself into yet another spiritual mess? How did I turn spiritual "success" into "failure" so quickly?

I sat there for a long time, sometimes reading my Bible, at other times praying, and all the time waiting for an answer. I don't remember exactly how it came to me, but it was clear. Reflecting on each of my significant moments of spiritual burnout, I saw a definite pattern. Each instance of collapse into spiritual failure was preceded by an ever-increasing preoccupation with people.

That day under the tree may well have been the most significant day of my life. I made a promise that going forward I would never allow myself to care more about the opinions of people than I did about the opinions of God. It changed my life. Making a similar decision will change yours as well.

## BEST FRIENDS

> And Saul's son Jonathan went to David at Horesh and helped him find strength in God.
>
> 1 Samuel 23:16

Throughout my spiritual life, I have had no shortage of people ready to give me both positive and negative input. Every time I have experienced spiritual burnout, there have been people ready with their assessment, judgment, or even criticism. Some have meant well, others have meant harm, but none of them mattered nearly as much as those who pointed me to God.

From my earliest days as a Christian, God has guided me to people who were God-centered and would help me find strength in God. I can still remember my first spiritual best friend. The inscription in his day planner described a man named Enoch, whose relationship with God was so close that God didn't allow him to die. Instead, God brought Enoch straight to heaven.

> Enoch walked faithfully with God; then he was no more, because God took him away.
>
> Genesis 5:24

God guided me to marry my wife, Gail, because she is a person who places great value on pleasing God and helping people, not performing for them. Without her, my relationship with God would probably have been sacrificed to selfish ambition years ago. Her guiding Scripture passage for me has always been Psalm 90, and she continually urges me to be satisfied with God rather than seeking the praise of people.

> Satisfy us in the morning with your unfailing love, that we may sing for joy and be glad all our days.
>
> Psalm 90:14

In the Bay Area Christian Church, where I serve as part of the leadership team, I am surrounded by men and women who have little interest in the politics of a church or a position. Their primary interest is in developing a passionate walk with God. Friendships in a spiritual family like this keep me focused, safe, and pleasing in God's sight.

I hope you will find your own "River," "Tree," and "Best Friends" to help you successfully navigate the turning points in your own life. When we make God our primary focus, being a part of a church is an exhilarating and inspiring experience. When God is our focus, we aren't afraid to be different or think differently. Together with our spiritually minded friends, we will fulfill the destinies to which God has called us. With this strength we can make God attractive and build churches that inspire the community and world around us.

As we move forward into our next chapter, we will examine yet another threat to our focus on God—emotion. We will learn how the emotional crises in our lives can distort our view of God and cause us to turn away from him. We will also see how we can understand and manage our emotions in a spiritual way, so they enhance rather than diminish our walk with God.

## DIVE DEEP: Pause and Reflect
Jot down notes you want to remember from each section

**3.1 WHEN PEOPLE BECOME GOD**
Overcoming the fear of being different
Numbers 14:24, Jonah 2:8, Romans 12:2, Jeremiah 1:4-5, Psalm 139:15-16, Acts 17:26-27

**3.2 IT'S OKAY TO BE DIFFERENT**

**3.3 THINK DIFFERENTLY**
Acts 24:25, 1 Samuel 3:4-8

**3.4 THINKING TRADITIONALLY**
2 Corinthians 3:17, Colossians 2:19, Colossians 2:20-23

**3.5 THE RIVER, THE TREE, AND BEST FRIENDS**
1 Kings 18:37
1. The River
Ezekiel 3:15

2. The Tree
1 Kings 19:4

3. Best Friends
1 Samuel 23:16, Genesis 5:24, Psalm 90:14

1 BIG TAKEAWAY:

Scan this QR code with your phone's camera to check out the latest resources on this chapter here

## CHAPTER FOUR:
# WHEN EMOTIONS BECOME GOD

*Increasing Our Emotional Awareness*

One definition of a religious experience is an encounter with the divine. At age nine I felt I had had such an experience when I first watched *Star Trek* and encountered Chief Science Officer Spock of the USS Enterprise. I began watching the show in the summer of 1969, right after moving to Kentwood, Michigan. The *TV Guide* listed its start time as 11:03 p.m., and each week I was somehow able to convince my parents to let me watch.

I was captivated by this emotionless "deity" who rejected feeling in favor of logic. Watching Spock handle himself was instructive. He convinced me that the best way to live life was logically and without emotion. In one episode, he explained that insults would only be effective if emotions were present.[10] This was pretty persuasive stuff for a young kid who was entering adolescence and didn't want his feelings to get hurt. What I didn't realize at the time was that I was learning a lesson in suppression, because as human beings we are actually emotional beings.

As the years have gone by, it has become clear to me that we frequently receive misleading information about dealing with and managing our emotions. These false views go largely undetected and uncorrected and therefore impact us throughout our lives. We become spouses, parents, and leaders without receiving much of an emotional education. We also become religious and join churches. All of these relationships require a fairly high level of emotional intelligence, but unless we pick it up on our own, we won't have it.

In the area of emotional education, religion in general and churches in particular are no more successful than their secular counterparts. Through my personal and leadership experience, I have learned the importance of emotional education in the church. When I first began working in the ministry during the 1980s, I was largely unaware of my own emotional state, let alone the emotional condition of others. This resulted in a failure on my part to understand those I led. I was emotionally tone-deaf—I could hear, but I wasn't able to listen.

All that changed when I began to struggle, suffer, and fail. During those times I had to search the depths of my soul to find my way back to God. I discovered that finding God was not only a spiritual journey, but also an emotional one. I found out that inside of me, as well as inside of others, were what the Bible calls "deep waters."

> The purposes of a person's heart are deep waters, but one who has insight draws them out.
>
> Proverbs 20:5

Although I may not have expressed—or even been aware of—the emotion I felt inside, it was being stored up in my heart. Every day, in all types of situations and relationships,

I was recording and archiving emotions that would eventually surface.

> A good man brings good things out of the good stored up in his heart, and an evil man brings evil things out of the evil stored up in his heart. For the mouth speaks what the heart is full of.
>
> Luke 6:45

I am grateful for the emotional education God has given me by walking with him. In recent years, I have come to understand that we need to develop our emotional awareness if we are to build an attractive relationship with God. The religious assumption that the spiritual will somehow overcome the emotional is incorrect. The spiritual and the emotional work together to make our relationship with God satisfying, complete, and inspiring.

If we fail to understand how they work together, we will become spiritually dry, boring, uninspired, and dead. In this environment, God will become unattractive to us. When God's influence and presence are absent from our lives, our emotions will become our god.

## HOW EMOTION BECOMES GOD

> Yet I hold this against you: You have forsaken the love you had at first.
>
> Revelation 2:4

After being a Christian for only a few months, I heard a particularly passionate sermon on Jesus' sacrifice on the cross. The speaker talked at length about the importance of being motivated and emotionally moved by the cross. I listened to and later reflected on this message. I didn't think I had that type of emotional connection with God. I was concerned enough to pick up the phone and call one of my friends in the church. I told him that I didn't have the heart response to the cross that the speaker had described earlier that morning.

His reply was genuine and well-meaning. He said, "Russ, not everyone will feel that way about the cross. If you understand and believe in what Jesus did for you, that is enough."

At the time I believed him, but I later discovered that my lack of an emotional response exposed my lack of emotional relationship with God. Over the years, I learned that a detached or distant response to the cross leads to spiritual powerlessness. Without an emotional connection to God, I was powerless. I could be easily tempted to love something or someone more than him. I was particularly vulnerable to anything or anyone who promised to fill the emptiness. I was walking around with a full Christian schedule of church attendance and religious duty, but an empty heart.

When we have a busy Christian life but feel unsatisfied, this means that our emotions have replaced God. We don't feel love for him or from him. I believe this is how Demas, a faithful friend of the apostle Paul, met his spiritual demise. Demas went from a heroic missionary to a man who loved the world more than God. He must have felt the emptiness that comes when we are emotionally disconnected. It is an emptiness of heart that made him, and will make us, vulnerable to another love.

> Do your best to come to me quickly, <u>for Demas, because he loved this world,</u> has deserted me and has gone to Thessalonica. Crescens has gone to Galatia, and Titus to Dalmatia.

2 Timothy 4:9-10

When our emotions become our god, they go searching for another love. These emotions manifest themselves under a number of names like anger, bitterness, cynicism, discouragement, despair, envy, jealousy, and the like. They are powerful enough to make us question the value of a relationship with God. This is the very question the psalmist Asaph was asking in Psalm 73.

> Surely God is good to Israel, to those who are pure in heart. But as for me, my feet had almost slipped; I had nearly lost my foothold. <u>For I envied</u> the arrogant when I saw the prosperity of the wicked.
>
> Psalm 73:1-3

Envy is certainly a sin, but it is also a powerful feeling that can cause us to question the value of staying faithful to God. Without an emotional connection to him, we begin to feel detached from God, and this envy—like any other emotion—can become god. Asaph described this detachment from God in Psalm 73:21.

> When my heart was grieved and my spirit embittered,
> I was senseless and ignorant; I was a brute
> beast before you.
>
> Psalm 73:21-22

Asaph shows us the path to victory over these deadly emotions when he turns his desire back to God. Only a deep intimacy can overcome the powerful emotions that would pull us away from him.

> Yet I am always with you; you hold me by my right hand. You guide me with your counsel, and afterward you will take me into glory. Whom have I in heaven but you? And earth has <u>nothing I desire besides you</u>.
>
> Psalm 73:23–25

Fundamentally, we must understand that being emotionally connected to God is essential if we are to keep our emotions from leading us astray—from becoming a type of god themselves.

> But as for me, <u>it is good to be near God</u>. I have made the Sovereign LORD my refuge; I will tell of all your deeds.
>
> Psalm 73:28

Few people consider emotions to be evil, but emotions may be the most insidious threat to our relationship with God. Indeed, most emotions are not evil, but they do go in search of satisfaction. If they are not focused on God, they will lead us astray. This is not to say we will never experience negative emotion, but that we can stay strong in the midst of these emotions by continuing to develop a deep and constant emotional connection to God—in other words, an intimate relationship with him.

## INTIMACY WITH GOD

Intimacy is rarely easy and never completely safe. The first place I felt comfortable experiencing intimacy was in music; music never ridiculed or rejected. Novelist and poet Victor Hugo once said, "Music expresses that which cannot be said, and on which it is impossible to be silent."[11] It was music that made me realize Mr. Spock didn't have a clue.

## CHAPTER FOUR: WHEN EMOTIONS BECOME GOD

I began to listen to my sister's music when I was a sophomore in high school, and it changed me. One of my favorite groups was made up of all women and they were called "The Emotions." Their music put me in touch with my own feelings, many of which I could not even describe or express but knew were present when I listened to the songs.

Scan to listen to a music playlist on this topic.

My clearest memories of high school and college are associated with music, almost as if my life had a soundtrack. I can still remember music being the most distinctive thing about walking into my college dorm as a freshman. Although the bands playing were as varied as the personalities of my college dorm mates, they all served the same purpose. Everyone was listening to music that helped him or her feel and express powerful and deep-seated emotions.

We had great discussions about our music. We talked about whom we liked, why we liked them, and in some cases, the importance of their influence on the world. In one of these talks, someone asked whether I listened to "The Boss." I said that I certainly did, sure that they were referring to Diana Ross who had recently released an album called *The Boss*. There were chuckles all around as my midwestern R&B sensibilities were educated to the fact that on the East Coast, "The Boss" was Bruce Springsteen.

Moments later, I was involved in a Bruce Springsteen symposium. We listened to album after album. Those who were with me interpreted the meaning of these songs and passionately proclaimed that no one wrote songs like Bruce.

It took me a long time to warm to his voice and sound, but there was no denying the emotion. He made an emotional connection with the listener on each album and was nothing short of legendary in his concert performances.

One of his songs describes the intimacy between a man and a woman, but is also an accurate expression of the connection God seeks with us. The song is called "Two Hearts" and whether you read the lyrics or listen to the song, you can hear the plea God makes to us to acknowledge our need for him.

> Sometimes it might seem like it was planned
> For you to roam empty hearted through this land
> Though the world turns you hard and cold
> There's one thing mister that I know
>
> That's if you think your heart is stone
> And that you're rough enough to whip this world alone
> Alone buddy there ain't no peace of mind
> That's why I'll keep searching till I find my special one
> Two hearts are better than one.[12]

What I get from these lyrics is that we are intimate beings in a world made cold by wickedness. Jesus teaches us this truth in Matthew 24:

> Because of the increase of wickedness, the love of most will grow cold.
>
> Matthew 24:12

Because of this coldness we can stifle, suppress, or otherwise silence the emotions that live in our hearts. Unless we overcome our fears and find a way to feel and express the emotions that live within us, we will never experience a relationship that truly satisfies. The emotions we keep protected behind numerous shields and defenses are the same emotions that can lead us to God. We have to stop being afraid of them. We need to become aware of our emotions, reach out, and share them so we can develop the powerful intimacy God has with his people. Two hearts will indeed prove to be better than one.

> He has raised up for his people a horn, the praise of all his faithful servants, of Israel, <u>the people close to his heart</u>. Praise the LORD.
>
> Psalm 148:14
>
> He tends his flock like a shepherd: He gathers the lambs in his arms and <u>carries them close to his heart</u>; he gently leads those that have young.
>
> Isaiah 40:11

What few people realize is that the whole point of salvation and being a Christian is to enjoy intimacy with God. This is what our hearts and emotions are constantly seeking and is not a side benefit or luxury experienced only by the fortunate few. This is what David was describing in Psalm 63 when he wrote from the desert that God's love for him was better than life.

> You, God, are my God, earnestly I seek you; I thirst for you, my whole being longs for you, in a dry and parched land where there is no water. I have seen you in the sanctuary and beheld your power and your glory. Because your love is better than life, my lips will glorify you.
>
> Psalm 63:1–3

David realized that the things of this world could not quench his constant thirst. He needed to experience a closeness to God so satisfying that his emotions would stop panting for something more. When we constantly want more, the different and the new, it is a sure sign that our thirst is unsatisfied and our emotions are trying to lead us to God.

> As the deer pants for streams of water, <u>so my soul pants for you, my God</u>. My soul thirsts for God, for the living God. When can I go and meet with God?
>
> Psalm 42:1–2

There are far too many of us living lives of—to use the words of Henry David Thoreau—quiet desperation.[13] We never discover who we are or what we are meant to do because we turn to people and things rather than to God. Life doesn't have to be this way.

Today is as good as any to begin our quest to develop intimacy with God—to awaken the song that lives within us. We need to understand our emotional selves—our true selves—and then seek the very real God to whom our emotions point. He is a God who is as real as—and yet more powerful than—the emotions we feel, and he can satisfy them completely.

## GOD IS REAL

> Job continued his discourse: "How I long for the months gone by, for the days when God watched over me, when his lamp shone on my head and by his light I walked through darkness! Oh, for the days when I was in my prime, <u>when God's intimate friendship blessed my house</u>, when the Almighty was still with me and my children

were around me, when my path was drenched with cream and the rock poured out for me streams of olive oil.

Job 29:1–6

God should be as real to us as our dearest friend. This is what I tell anyone who asks me how to pray. I tell them that we should talk to God in the same way we talk to a close friend. While there is a place for the sacred language of majesty and awe, intimacy comes when God is as real as a close friend. This is how he spoke with the men and women in Scripture who became his best friends.

> The LORD would speak to Moses face to face, <u>as one speaks to a friend</u>. Then Moses would return to the camp, but his young aide Joshua son of Nun did not leave the tent.

Exodus 33:11

Their faith did not merely lead to membership in a tribe, nation, or church. For them, faith was more than behavioral change or obedience to a set of rules. Their faith led to an intimate friendship with God.

> And the scripture was fulfilled that says, "Abraham believed God, and it was credited to him as righteousness," <u>and he was called God's friend</u>.

James 2:23

Building a friendship with God requires that we understand him. We can't do all the talking. We have to do some listening. We must make certain the conversation is flowing in both directions. When this happens, I guarantee we will hear some things we don't like. The relationship will be tested.

> The LORD your God is testing you <u>to find out whether you love him</u> with all your heart and with all your soul.
>
> Deuteronomy 13:3

We will come face-to-face with the reality that God's expectations and ours are different. He will make decisions we don't agree with, despite our arguments to the contrary. In those moments, the unsettling reality that he is the decision-maker in the relationship becomes clear. We will question him and receive answers we don't like. We will doubt and distrust him when he takes us down paths that make little sense and provide no relief.

In all of this relationship turbulence, we will experience relationship strain. The struggle will always be worth it, but it will require a daily decision to keep walking with God. Through it all, we will be tested, and we will discover whether the two of us can truly agree to walk together in this life.

> Do two walk together unless they have agreed to do so?
>
> Amos 3:3

In the Bible, Jacob is someone who struggled in his relationship with God in this very way. He liked the benefits, but not the obedience involved in having a relationship with God. He deceived his brother into forfeiting the blessings that came with being the firstborn. He developed a weak character by regularly looking for shortcuts.

This deceptiveness became the unfinished business of Jacob's life. We'll discuss unfinished business in depth in the next chapter, but for now what's important to note is that no matter what Jacob did or how successful he became, the deceitfulness of his character threatened to unravel his life. God knew this and chose to engage him in a very painful struggle. This struggle produced real, transformative, and lasting change.

## THE STRUGGLE WILL BE REAL

> <u>So Jacob was left alone,</u> and a man wrestled with him till daybreak. When the man saw that he could not overpower him, he touched the socket of Jacob's hip so that <u>his hip was wrenched as he wrestled with the man.</u>
>
> Genesis 32:24–25

Jacob had been involved with God all of his life, but he never really learned to rely on him. Instead, he counted on his ability to deceive and manipulate people to get his own way. Until he dealt with the unfinished business of his deceitful character, his relationship with God could never be genuine or intimate.

God decided that the only way to change Jacob was to take the fight to him. He wrestled Jacob physically in the same way he might wrestle with us spiritually. The struggle was intense for Jacob and the struggle will be just as difficult when God takes the fight to us. He will use every relationship, circumstance, and event in our lives to resolve our unfinished business and inspire us to turn to him.

We will learn that God is much more than a quiet time of prayer and Bible study. He is much more than church attendance or a willingness to volunteer. He is a God with a very tangible and real involvement in our lives that will be felt as he changes us.

## THE CHANGE WILL BE TRANSFORMATIVE

> Then the man said, "Let me go, for it is daybreak." But Jacob replied, "I will not let you go unless you bless me." The man asked him, "What is your name?" "Jacob," he answered. Then the man said, "Your name will no longer be Jacob, but Israel, because <u>you have struggled with God and with humans and have overcome</u>."
>
> Genesis 32:26–28

Jacob experienced more than a change of behavior; he experienced transformative change, which is a change of heart. Throughout Jacob's life, God tried to develop an intimate relationship with him, but Jacob preferred to rely on himself. When the wrestling began, Jacob fought fiercely and would not let go, saying, "I will not let you go unless you bless me." Jacob thought he had won, but in fact, God had won. For the first time, Jacob was clinging to God and would not let go.

This match was symbolic of Jacob's lifelong wrestling with God. The name Jacob means "deceiver," but through his struggle with man and God, he became Israel, which means "one who prevails with God." Through the struggles of his life, Jacob experienced a transformative change that had a lasting impact on him and his entire family, as well as on all of us today.

**CHAPTER FOUR: WHEN EMOTIONS BECOME GOD**

## THE CHANGE WILL LAST

> Then he blessed Joseph and said, "May the God before whom my fathers Abraham and Isaac walked faithfully, <u>the God who has been my shepherd all my life</u> to this day, <u>the Angel who has delivered me from all harm</u>—may he bless these boys. May they be called by my name and the names of my fathers Abraham and Isaac, and may they increase greatly upon the earth."
>
> Genesis 48:15–16

The struggle is real, the change is real, and the blessing is real when we truly walk with God. There were difficult and dark moments in Jacob's life, but as he looked back from the perspective of old age, he could see that there had been lasting change. He had dealt with his unfinished business. He had become and remained Israel, and had passed on his faith and relationship with God to his children and grandchildren.

In the next chapter, we'll begin to identify our own unfinished emotional business. Unfinished business in our lives can cause us to doubt God's care and give us a false impression of who he is. We'll also learn how to handle the emotional crises that threaten to undermine our relationship with God, so that we can handle the difficulties of life with faith and endurance.

**HE'S NOT WHO YOU THINK HE IS**

## DIVE DEEP: Pause and Reflect
Jot down notes you want to remember from each section

**4.1** WHEN EMOTIONS BECOME GOD
Proverbs 20:5, Luke 6:45

**4.2** HOW EMOTION BECOMES GOD
Revelation 2:4, 2 Timothy 4:9-10, Psalm 73:1-3, 21-22, 23-25, 28

**4.5** THE STRUGGLE WILL BE REAL
Genesis 32:24-25

**4.3** INTIMACY WITH GOD
Matthew 24:12, Psalm 148:14, Isaiah 40:11, Psalm 63:1-3, Psalm 42:1-2

**4.6** THE CHANGE WILL BE TRANSFORMATIVE
Genesis 32:26-28

**4.4** GOD IS REAL
Job 29:1-6, Exodus 33:11, James 2:23, Deuteronomy 13:3, Amos 3:3

**4.7** THE CHANGE WILL LAST
Genesis 48:15-16

1 BIG TAKEAWAY:

Which emotions do I feel the most on a daily basis?

Happy  Sad  Afraid  Ashamed  Angry

Scan this QR code with your phone's camera to check out the latest resources on this chapter here

# CHAPTER FIVE:
# WHY WE DOUBT GOD

*Identifying Our Unfinished Emotional Business*

> Consider it pure joy, my brothers, whenever you face trials of many kinds, because you know that the testing of your faith produces perseverance. <u>Let perseverance finish its work</u> so that you may be mature and complete, not lacking anything.
>
> James 1:2–4

During a difficult period of my life, I read a book called *Spiritual Maturity* by J. Oswald Sanders. There was a chapter entitled "The Undiscouraged Perseverance of God" that provided an in-depth study of how God brought about transformative change in the life of Jacob. That chapter opened my mind to the truth that God will persevere with us until we deal with our unfinished business. I think this is an important truth for both the individual and the church community to embrace.

Unfinished business refers to past behaviors and issues that are shaping our present actions in unhealthy ways. The Bible describes this unfinished business as "unplowed ground."

> Sow righteousness for yourselves, reap the fruit of unfailing love, and break up your unplowed ground; for it is time to seek the LORD, until he comes and showers his righteousness on you.
>
> Hosea 10:12

Every day, people take jobs, get married, have children, and join churches with a great deal of their personal business unfinished. Eventually, these issues surface and can become dangerous for both the individual and for all who are in relationship with them. I have seen both sides of this dilemma. My own unfinished business has negatively affected people. I have also seen the lives of many people damaged by others who were unwilling to deal with their own unfinished business.

When we refuse to resolve our unfinished business, we are like the character Martin Riggs in the movie *Lethal Weapon*. *Lethal Weapon* was released in March of 1987 and at the risk of dating myself, I will readily admit that I was among the first to see it. Danny Glover played the role of a veteran detective named Roger Murtaugh. His younger partner, Martin Riggs, was played by Mel Gibson.

Although he is a fictional character, Martin Riggs is a useful example of someone with unfinished business. He had a great many unresolved emotional issues, which caused him to live on the edge. Roger Murtaugh is the older and more stable character, who has a family and is looking forward to retirement. When Murtaugh realizes that being partnered with Riggs could cost him his life, he laments the partnership by lamenting that God must hate him. Riggs retorts to just hate God back—that's what he does and it works for him.

As humorous as Riggs' response is, it can be an all-too-real example of what happens when our unfinished business inserts itself into our spiritual lives. It can turn us against God, our spouse, our children, or our church. Unresolved emotional issues are dangerous for those seeking God.

## IDENTIFYING OUR UNFINISHED EMOTIONAL BUSINESS

> Absalom <u>never said a word</u> to Amnon, either good or bad; <u>he hated Amnon</u> because he had disgraced his sister Tamar.
>
> 2 Samuel 13:22

One of the most disturbing stories in the Bible involves Absalom, Amnon, and their sister, Tamar. If you go back and read the story in 2 Samuel 13, you'll find that Absalom never resolved his hatred toward Amnon and eventually even had him murdered.

The presence of unresolved emotional issues is a warning sign that we have unfinished business. Whether we are seeking God, seeking relationships, or seeking to become part of a church community, unresolved emotional issues can unravel any progress we hope to make. They can upset, defile, and even destroy the spiritual and emotional fabric of our lives. If we get specific and ask for God's help, these weaknesses can be turned into strengths. Examine the following areas of possible unfinished business that might be manifesting themselves in your life and seek help for what applies to you.

### 1. UNFINISHED SPIRITUAL BUSINESS

We won't experience much growth in our intimacy with God if we only deal with the superficial issues in our lives.

We have to take a deep look into our hearts and characters to experience lasting growth and change. This means overcoming our fear of discussing the spiritual issues that trouble us. We should regularly share with our closest spiritual relationships our doubts, questions, and even our temptations to abandon the faith. We must also overcome our fear of discussing sin, especially the concealed sins that eat away at our heart and soul. We must resolve our unfinished spiritual business if we hope to thrive spiritually and renew our attraction to God.

**2. UNFINISHED FAMILY BUSINESS**

Am I running from or refusing to resolve any family relationship problems? Everyone has some type of family dysfunction that, if left unresolved, will affect their ability to build a healthy relationship with God and other people.

In most cases, these issues are more easily resolved than we might believe. However, sometimes certain behaviors may pose an emotional or physical threat that makes resolution difficult or unsafe. In every case, we need to make certain that we identify unfinished business in our family and resolve it where possible. In situations where face-to-face resolution is impossible, we can still seek help in safe relationships (friends, counseling, etc.).

**3. UNFINISHED RELATIONSHIP BUSINESS**

Do I have a pattern of failure in friendships that I refuse to acknowledge or deal with? Unless we acknowledge the unhealthy patterns in building our relationships and learn to build better, we are likely to repeat our mistakes.

**4. UNFINISHED DATING, ENGAGEMENT, OR MARRIAGE BUSINESS**

Do I have a pattern of distrust in my relationships with the opposite sex? Rejection, betrayal, or abusive experiences in romantic relationships can undermine our ability to build spiritual dating relationships in God's family. These experiences can leave us distrusting God's willingness or ability to protect us. Resolving these issues is essential for God to be able to fulfill our dreams of intimacy with him as well as the person who is meant to be our spouse.

### 5. UNFINISHED EMOTIONAL BUSINESS

Do I have a mental health issue for which I have not sought diagnosis or treatment? Do I believe that having a relationship with God makes mental health care optional? We must understand that having a relationship with God or being a spiritual person does not automatically correct mental health problems. Leaving mental health care needs unresolved is dangerous to the individual as well as to all those with whom they attempt to build relationships in a spiritual community.

### 6. UNFINISHED CAREER OR FINANCIAL BUSINESS

Do I have a pattern of job loss or financial trouble that I have not yet acknowledged? Developing a relationship with God or joining a church does not suddenly resolve or fix these issues. We must address this area of our character or it will surface again in our lives. If unaddressed, these issues can undermine our spiritual work in our relationships with God and people, and the stability of our own lives.

### 7. UNFINISHED RELIGIOUS BUSINESS

Sometimes we have a bad religious experience with a church and then rebound to another church. When we arrive at this new church, everything seems so much better—until something happens there. Then we go on the rebound again. Church shopping or hopping might simply be the result of a refusal to deal with our own unfinished religious business. Perhaps we have unrealistic expectations of what a church can and should be, or even unrealistic expectations of God.

If you're not sure whether unfinished business is affecting your spiritual life, let's take a look at some of the most common warning signs.

## COMMON WARNING SIGNS OF UNFINISHED EMOTIONAL BUSINESS

### Unrealistic Expectations of the Church

> Others, like seed sown on rocky places, hear the word and at once receive it with joy. But since they have no root, they last only a short time. When trouble or persecution comes because of the word, they quickly fall away.
>
> Mark 4:16–17

Those of us who have unfinished business in our lives will usually be drawn to God or to the church at some point. We often come to the family of God with the same joy that Jesus attributed to the seed that fell on rocky soil in Mark 4:16–17. This joy lasts as long as we have no challenges. But as soon as difficulties arise, we fall away. We leave God and his people. Why? I believe it is because our initial commitment is superficial and based on unrealistic expectations of the church.

There are six common unrealistic expectations that I see people bringing into their church relationships:

1. They will solve my problems.
2. They will never let me down.
3. They will love me perfectly.
4. They will make my dreams come true.
5. They will make everything right.

6. They will always make me happy.

While God can certainly fulfill all of these expectations,

people cannot. Unfortunately, most people with unfinished business have not developed the type of mature relationship with God that meets their needs. As a result, they become preoccupied with human relationships, and at some point, one or more of their expectations go unfulfilled.

When we turn to God and decide to join his people in a church, we need to remember that, as great as these people might be, *they are not God*. We should never set our hopes *on*

the people but share our hope *with* them. Together we can seek and walk with the God who can fulfill all of our expectations.

### Unhealthy Emotional Dependence

> For what we preach is not ourselves, but Jesus Christ as Lord, and ourselves as your servants for Jesus' sake.
>
> 2 Corinthians 4:5

When we have unfinished business, we can easily develop an unhealthy emotional dependence on people. This is why the Bible admonishes leaders to preach Christ and not themselves. The point is to keep the focus on God and not on fallible human beings. There are two groups of people who can develop unhealthy emotional dependency issues and have to be especially careful in this area.

The first group are those people with unfinished business who then look to human relationships to heal their emotional pain, rather than go to God for healing. If we are tempted to build flawed relationships based on unhealthy emotional dependence, we need to make that clear to our closest friends, so they can help us establish healthy patterns. We must also devote ourselves to developing a deeply intimate relationship with God. When necessary, we should not hesitate to seek professional help.

Leaders make up the second group that must carefully avoid building relationships with an unhealthy emotional dependence. Leaders must constantly examine their motives. When their desire for human attention is greater than their desire for God, they become a magnet for those who are seeking a human relationship to heal their emotional pain.

### Unhelpful Relationship Disconnection

> Blessed is the one who always trembles before God, but whoever hardens their heart falls into trouble.
>
> Proverbs 28:14

There can be events in life that are so painful that we disconnect from the source of the pain. If we do not reconnect, we can develop a relationship pattern that leaves us in a state of permanent disconnection. This disconnection can make us emotionally tone-deaf. As a result, we simply do not read other people well. We can lack the empathy and compassion to listen. We may not be able to hear what they are saying or what they are feeling. This disconnection can cause us to struggle to develop intimacy in personal relationships. Those we love may feel alone, even when we are with them.

In short, if we harden ourselves to the difficult and painful events in our lives, an unhealthy relationship disconnection can develop. If we enter into a relationship with God or his people without understanding, acknowledging, and attempting to change this, our spiritual experiences will be disappointing and frustrating.

**Undisciplined Ambition for Self**

> Who is wise and understanding among you? Let them show it by their good life, by deeds done in the humility that comes from wisdom. But if you harbor bitter envy and selfish ambition in your hearts, do not boast about it or deny the truth. Such "wisdom" does not come down from heaven but is earthly, unspiritual, demonic. For where you have envy and selfish ambition, <u>there you find disorder</u> and every evil practice.
>
> James 3:13–16

I used to think that once I became a Christian and part of the church, altruistic ideals would reign in my heart. I was surprised to discover in myself, and in others, an enormous desire to succeed in the sometimes highly political and social ecosystem of the church. Membership in the church did not end my search for significance, success, and human validation.

The undisciplined ambition for self lives on until we develop a relationship with God that can quiet the storm. Unless it is shaped and disciplined by the power of God, the church can become a human outlet for selfish ambition. If we have not found contentment in God, we will compete and battle in the church as much as any non-believer will compete and battle in the world. This self-seeking will continue as long as our relationship with God is dissatisfying. In our search for significance, we can become the people most likely to debate, divide, and eventually destroy the church. We need to deal with our unfinished business, so that we can find contentment in God and allow those around us to experience it as well.

**Chronic Discouragement and Disappointment**

> A happy heart makes the face cheerful, but <u>heartache crushes the spirit</u>.
>
> Proverbs 15:13

One of the most devastating consequences of unfinished business is a chronic sense of discouragement and disappointment. I have seen it in my own life as well as in the lives of others. A happy heart remains elusive as long as our heartache is unresolved.

Perhaps you feel that your unfinished business is too difficult to overcome and you don't want to revisit such heartbreak. This is understandable, but resolving unfinished business doesn't require extraordinary drama. It all starts with God and the fact that he draws especially close to the brokenhearted.

> <u>The Lord is close to the brokenhearted</u> and saves those who are crushed in spirit.
>
> Psalm 34:18

With God so close, anything is possible—including the resolution of our unfinished business. We should trust and rely on him to help us take whatever action is necessary to move on. He can give us the power to forgive and make peace with every person and memory so that our unfinished business no longer clouds our future with disappointment or discouragement.

## EMOTIONAL CRISES

> But when you ask, you must believe and not doubt, because <u>the one who doubts is like a wave of the sea, blown and tossed by the wind</u>. That person should not expect to receive anything from the Lord. Such a person is <u>double-minded</u>, <u>unstable in all they do</u>.
>
> James 1:6–8

On most occasions, it isn't the unfinished business of the past that threatens to undermine our relationship with God, but some emotional crisis of the present. Negative emotions surface during inevitable moments when our lives become filled with pain. These feelings are so strong that unless we understand and process them correctly, they can create doubt that eventually undermines our faith in God.

More people lose their faith in God due to an emotional crisis than they do because of any "facts" that disprove his existence or his truth. In the Bible, Satan usually attacks a person's faith through his or her emotions. In the case of Eve, Satan (in the form of a serpent) first causes her to doubt God's trustworthiness. Satan does not present facts. He merely creates doubt, which unleashes unhealthy emotions.

> Now the serpent was more crafty than any of the wild animals the Lord God had made. He said to the woman, "<u>Did God really say</u>, 'You must not eat from any tree in the garden'?" The woman said to the serpent, "We may

eat fruit from the trees in the garden, but God did say, 'You must not eat fruit from the tree that is in the middle of the garden, and you must not touch it, or you will die.'" "<u>You will not certainly die</u>," the serpent said to the woman. "<u>For God knows</u> that when you eat from it your eyes will be opened, and you will be like God, knowing good and evil."

Genesis 3:1–5

Satan makes Eve think that God is holding out on her. She then notices three things—each very emotional—about the fruit Satan is encouraging her to eat. She notices that it is good, pleasing, and desirable.

When the woman saw that the fruit of the tree was <u>good for food</u> and <u>pleasing to the eye</u>, and also <u>desirable for gaining wisdom</u>, she took some and ate it. She also gave some to her husband, who was with her, and he ate it.

Genesis 3:6

Satan did not seek to prove anything, he merely encouraged Eve to see God through her emotions. Now let's take a look at Job, a person well known for receiving devastating emotional blows.

"Does Job fear God for nothing?" Satan replied. "Have you not put a hedge around him and his household and everything he has? You have blessed the work of his hands, so that his flocks and herds are spread throughout the land. But stretch out your hand and <u>strike everything he has</u>, and <u>he will surely curse you to your face</u>."

Job 1:9–11

Satan doesn't argue about God's existence or trustworthiness with Job. He creates a crisis and then lets the emotions do their work. When the first attack on his family and possessions fails to destroy Job's faith, Satan attacks his health.

> Then the Lord said to Satan, "Have you considered my servant Job? There is no one on earth like him; he is blameless and upright, a man who fears God and shuns evil. And he still maintains his integrity, though you incited me against him to ruin him without any reason." "Skin for skin!" Satan replied. "<u>A man will give all he has for his own life</u>. But stretch out your hand and strike his flesh and bones, <u>and he will surely curse you to your face</u>."
>
> Job 2:3–5

Each time Satan attacks, he targets Job's emotions as well as the emotions of those on whom Job depends. Job is able to hold on, but his wife breaks down in the face of crisis.

> Then Job took a piece of broken pottery and scraped himself with it as he sat among the ashes. His wife said to him, "Are you still maintaining your integrity? Curse God and die!" He replied, "You are talking like a foolish woman. Shall we accept good from God, and not trouble?" In all this, Job did not sin in what he said.
>
> Job 2:8–10

Who hasn't experienced a moment like Job's wife did? When we look at our lives and see a mess, we believe God is responsible and blame him for the cruelness of fate. He is responsible for the roll of the dice, for time and chance dealing us the devastating blows of an emotional crisis or personal tragedy.

Emotions are too powerful to be ignored. They can change how we see God. When life is going well, we generally feel good about him—or at least apathetic. When things go poorly, our feelings toward God usually change. Those good feelings toward him turn negative and, where there was apathy in good times, we can now feel rage.

> A person's own folly leads to their ruin, yet their heart rages against the Lord.
>
> Proverbs 19:3

The failure to deal properly with our emotions can cost us our faith. It can twist how we see God and cause us to turn away from him. Jesus understood this and warned his friend and disciple Peter that Satan would not dissuade him from believing with logical arguments, but with an emotional crisis.

> "Simon, Simon, Satan has asked to <u>sift you as wheat</u>. But I have prayed for you, Simon, that <u>your faith may not fail</u>. And when you have turned back, strengthen your brothers."
>
> Luke 22:31-32

The bottom line is that emotion replaces God when an emotional crisis causes us to turn our backs on him. What are some of these emotional crises that can break down our will and endurance and threaten to take away our faith?

1. Death of a loved one
2. Financial or job loss
3. Physical or emotional health challenges
4. Physical or intellectual disabilities

5. Marriage or family breakdown
6. Relationship breakup or estrangement
7. Chronic discouragement from personal failure
8. Unanswered prayers and failure to receive God's help
9. Transitions and life passages (i.e., mid-life crisis)

Identifying our unfinished emotional business and any emotional crises in our lives is an important step toward dropping our assumptions about God. Now that we have identified some common reasons we doubt God, we will move on to discovering how to develop a satisfying relationship with him by rebuilding our emotional lives.

**CHAPTER FIVE: WHY WE DOUBT GOD**

# DIVE DEEP: Pause and Reflect
Jot down notes you want to remember from each section

## 5.1 WHY WE DOUBT GOD
Identifying Our emotional unfinished business
James 1:2-4, Hosea 10:12, 2 Samuel 13:22

1. Unfinished Spiritual Business

2. Unfinished Family Business

3. Unfinished Relationship Business

4. Unfinished Dating, Engagement, or Marriage Business

5. Unfinished Emotional Business

6. Unfinished Career or Financial Business

7. Unfinished Religious Business

Identifying Our Unfinished Emotional Business

### 5.2b UNHELPFUL RELATIONSHIP DISCONNECT
Proverbs 28:14

### 5.2c UNDISCIPLINED AMBITION FOR SELF
James 3:13-16

### 5.2d CHRONIC DISCOURAGEMENT AND DISAPPOINTMENT
Proverbs 15:13, Psalm 34:18

## 5.2 UNREALISTIC EXPECTATIONS OF THE CHURCH
Mark 4:16-17

### 5.2e EMOTIONAL CRISES
James 1:6-8, Genesis 3:1-5, Genesis 3:6, Job 1:9-11, Job 2:3-5, Job 2:8-10, Proverbs 19:3, Luke 22:31-32

### 5.2a UNHEALTHY EMOTIONAL DEPENDENCE
2 Corinthians 4:5

1 BIG TAKEAWAY:

Scan this QR code with your phone's camera to check out the latest resources on this chapter here

## CHAPTER SIX:
# HOW GOD BECOMES SATISFYING

*Rebuilding Our Emotional Lives*

> <u>Here are the stages in the journey</u> of the Israelites when they came out of Egypt by divisions under the leadership of Moses and Aaron. At the Lord's command Moses recorded <u>the stages in their journey</u>. This is their journey by stages:
>
> Numbers 33:1–2

We have invested a fair amount of time examining and understanding our emotional journey as it relates to our spiritual lives. We began by developing an understanding of the relationship between our emotions and God. We learned that without an intimate relationship with God, our emotions will dominate our lives.

Intimacy with God can appear to be a mystical, ethereal, and almost unreachable state of relationship, so we studied the Scriptures and learned that God is indeed real. He moves, works, and involves himself in our daily lives through events, circumstances, and people. He is understandable and lovable.

It is precisely because our relationship with God is real that we experience his spiritual prompting to deal with our unfinished business. The unfinished business of our lives allows emotions of the past to interfere with our relationships with God, his church, and people around us. Dealing with our unfinished business sets us free to experience a new and unencumbered life of intimacy, connection, and satisfaction.

Remember that "emotional crisis" was the final impediment to building a healthy relationship with God and people. We learned that Satan's attack on our faith is not primarily through logical arguments against God or Scripture. His primary attack is on our emotional life, in the hope of breaking down our endurance and causing us to give up.

The good news is that God is capable of helping us overcome emotional scars and conquer emotional attacks. The victory begins and ends by completing two final steps that allow us to walk with God. The first step is to take an emotional inventory. The second and final step is to rebuild our damaged emotions. Let's begin by taking an emotional inventory.

## TAKING AN EMOTIONAL INVENTORY

An emotional inventory helps us understand where we are on the emotional spectrum. What are our strengths and our weaknesses? How do we interpret, process, and express our feelings? Based on our **emotional history**, each of us has developed an **emotional spectrum** that provides us with the capability to understand and express our feelings. If we have a **limited emotional spectrum, we will lack breadth and diversity in our feelings.** In that case, we will often find our relationships with God and people superficial, narrow, limited, and dissatisfying. On the other hand, when we have an **expansive emotional spectrum,** our relationships with God and people are deep, multifaceted, ever-growing, and fulfilling.

Because too few of us explore our emotional makeup, we don't realize how expansive or limited our capabilities might be. This is why taking an emotional inventory can be helpful. Let's look at some terms to help us understand what stage of the emotional journey we are on and what steps we need to take next in our relationship with God to make progress.

### 1. Emotionally Defensive

Return home, my daughters; <u>I am too old</u> to have another husband. <u>Even if I thought there was still hope for me</u>—even if I had a husband tonight and then gave birth to sons—would you wait until they grew up? Would you remain unmarried for them? No, my daughters. <u>It is more bitter for me than for you</u>, because <u>the Lord's hand has gone out against me</u>!"

Ruth 1:12–13

We become emotionally defensive when we feel hurt by God or someone else. This is the condition in which Naomi found herself when she spoke the words recorded in Ruth 1:12–13. After losing her husband and sons, she didn't want to make any more emotional connections. This is exactly how we feel when we have experienced a great deal of pain. What can we do when we find ourselves being emotionally defensive? There are some important lessons in the next part of this passage:

## CHAPTER SIX: HOW GOD BECOMES SATISFYING

> At this they wept aloud again. Then Orpah kissed her mother-in-law good-bye, <u>but Ruth clung to her.</u> "Look," said Naomi, "your sister-in-law is going back to her people and her gods. <u>Go back</u> with her." But Ruth replied, "<u>Don't urge me to leave you or to turn back from you.</u> Where you go I will go, and where you stay I will stay. Your people will be my people and your God my God. Where you die I will die, and there I will be buried. May the LORD deal with me, be it ever so severely, if anything but death separates you and me." When Naomi realized that Ruth was determined to go with her, she stopped urging her.
>
> Ruth 1:14–18

When we find ourselves being emotionally defensive, we need two things to restore our trust in relationships: friends who will not allow our defensiveness to drive them away and a relationship with God that helps us to trust these friends.

### 2. Emotionally Detached

> When Simon Peter saw this, he fell at Jesus' knees and said, "<u>Go away from me, Lord</u>; <u>I am a sinful man</u>!"
>
> Luke 5:8

Have you ever grown tired of feeling and simply shut down? When we grow weary of feeling, we don't want anyone to make us feel—not even God. Like Peter, we resist and pull away whenever God tries to get close to us. We especially hate it when he makes us aware of our sin because we already feel so terribly guilty.

If we prefer being emotionally detached, the good news is that we are not alone. This was exactly Peter's situation when he met Jesus. He told Jesus to go away because he felt too sinful to have a relationship with him. Have you ever felt too sinful to have a relationship with God or another person? When we are feeling emotionally detached and unworthy of relationships, we need a friend to do for us what Jesus did for Peter.

> Then Jesus said to Simon, "<u>Don't be afraid</u>; from now on <u>you will catch men</u>."
>
> Luke 5:10

Jesus told Peter two things: First, don't be afraid. If we are emotionally detached, we must rely on God to help us overcome our fear of feeling. We have to trust that feeling our feelings will improve our relationship with God and people, and will also make our lives more satisfying and encouraging.

The second thing Jesus did was point Peter away from his guilt and toward his purpose. Jesus knew that a sinful man transformed could be an inspiration to others to seek God. Simon Peter was a fisherman and Jesus told him that from that point on, he would no longer catch fish, but people. His new purpose would be to bring people to God.

Jesus turned Peter's negative into a positive. Those of us who are emotionally detached need a friend like Jesus, and when they come into our lives, we need to listen to them.

### 3. Emotionally Immature

> "Pardon me, my lord," Gideon replied, "but how can I save Israel? My clan is the weakest in Manasseh, and <u>I am the least</u> in my family."
>
> Judges 6:15

Those of us who are emotionally immature are afraid to grow up. We are afraid to take on responsibility. We see ourselves as the weakest and the least. Gideon was just like this, and what God told him to solve his problem can also apply to us.

> The Lord answered, "<u>I will be with you</u>, and you will strike down all the Midianites."
>
> Judges 6:16

God didn't argue with the fact that Gideon was the weakest or the least. He told him that it didn't matter because he was going to help him. Emotional immaturity is not some mysterious limiting condition that cannot be overcome. Emotional immaturity is a decision to live without relying on God. If we change that decision, he will give us the inner strength we need. Then dealing with our emotions and responsibilities will be much easier.

### 4. Emotionally Insecure

> <u>David was afraid of the Lord that day</u> and said, "How can the ark of the Lord ever come to me?"
>
> 2 Samuel 6:9

When we are emotionally insecure, we are afraid. We can feel this way in our relationship with God or with people. Fortunately for us, one of the greatest men of God in the Bible experienced fear and insecurity in his relationship with God. We have an example of his fear in 2 Samuel 6:9. When David saw God put a man to death for what he considered a minor infraction, it frightened him so much that he didn't want God's presence around him any longer.

Have you ever felt afraid of God? I know I have. When I was afraid, I became emotionally insecure. I didn't want to talk to him, trust him, or obey him. I wanted to take control of everything in my life. When I overcame my insecurity with God, I became secure enough to build relationships with others.

What makes us afraid in our relationship with God? To get you started, I have listed several things I have experienced myself. Feel free to add to the list. I've been...

1. Afraid he won't answer prayers.
2. Afraid he won't forgive my sins.
3. Afraid he will punish me for my sins.
4. Afraid he doesn't care.
5. Afraid he wants me to suffer.
6. Afraid he won't leave me alone and let me live my life.
7. _____
8. _____
9. _____
10. _____

When we are emotionally insecure, we can feel a variation on all these themes in our relationships with people. What can we do to overcome our emotional insecurity? The best thing we can do is talk to God the way David did in Psalm 30. This is a clear example of how he must have overcome his insecurity in 2 Samuel 6.

> Lord my God, I called to you for help, and you healed me. You, Lord, brought me up from the realm of the dead; you

spared me from going down to the pit. Sing the praises of the Lord, you his faithful people; praise his holy name. For his anger lasts only a moment, but his favor lasts a lifetime; weeping may stay for the night, but rejoicing comes in the morning. When I felt secure, I said, "I will never be shaken."

Psalm 30:2–6

David's first priority was finding security in his relationship with God, because when he was secure with God, he could walk securely among men. David called to God for help, healing, and an understanding of his constant love and favor. As he talked with God, he deepened his understanding and confidence that God was on his side, which made him feel secure. This is exactly how we must pray and walk with God to overcome our own emotional insecurity.

### 5. Emotionally Numb

Lord, they came to you <u>in their distress</u>; when you disciplined them, they could <u>barely whisper a prayer</u>.

Isaiah 26:16

I can clearly remember moments of such stress, strain, and pain that I didn't feel I had the strength to move forward one more inch. I was emotionally, spiritually, physically, and mentally numb. What can we do when we have reached this point? How can we proceed when we don't have any energy, optimism, or reason for hope? When we are so beaten down and exhausted that we can barely whisper, we need to make that whisper a prayer.

We must pray to have the desire to keep on believing. During these moments, we need to pray for the desire to do what is right because we feel a much stronger inclination to do what is wrong. When we are emotionally numb, we can't fake it with God. We have to beg him for the desire to fight. Believe me, he will give it to us. He gave it to an emotionally numb Jeremiah, who had grown weary with the spiritual battle.

> You deceived me, Lord, and I was deceived; you overpowered me and prevailed. I am ridiculed all day long; everyone mocks me.
>
> Jeremiah 20:7

Jeremiah was worn down and made it clear that he thought God had deceived him and made his life miserable, but that didn't stop God. Even in the midst of Jeremiah's complaint, God stoked the fires of motivation in his heart.

> But if I say, "I will not mention his word or speak anymore in his name," his word is in my heart like a fire, a fire shut up in my bones. I am weary of holding it in; indeed, I cannot.
>
> Jeremiah 20:9

We need to trust that God will—even in the midst of our complaint—unleash the fires of motivation in our hearts and revive us again if we just keep talking to him.

## EMOTIONAL REBUILDING

> As for everyone who comes to me and hears my words and puts them into practice, I will show you what they are like. They are like a man building a house, who dug

down deep and laid the foundation on rock. When a flood came, the torrent struck that house but could not shake it, because it was well built. But the one who hears my words and does not put them into practice is like a man who built a house on the ground without a foundation. The moment the torrent struck that house, it collapsed and its destruction was complete."

Luke 6:47–49

The Bible talks a great deal more about building than most people believe. I mention this because many people come to God expecting a quick miracle that will make everything better. What the Bible actually emphasizes is a long-term view of life—building. Luke 6:47–49 makes clear that those who refuse to take the time to dig down deep and lay the foundation on rock will inevitably experience collapse. In many cases, this collapse will be both spiritual and emotional.

My personal and leadership experience has given me the opportunity to see what both the storms and the collapses look like. Everyone experiences storms, but not everyone has to experience collapse. Those whose lives collapse almost always have ignored the emotional aspect of their spiritual lives—they were not willing to dig down deep. Rebuilding our emotional lives will allow us to grow our character as we walk with God and develop our strength from the inside out.

> I pray that out of his glorious riches he may strengthen you with power through his Spirit <u>in your inner being</u>, so that Christ may dwell in your hearts through faith. And I pray that you, being <u>rooted and established in love</u>, may have power, together with all the Lord's holy people, to <u>grasp</u> how wide and long and high and deep is the love of Christ, and to <u>know this love</u> that surpasses knowledge—that you may be filled to the measure of all the fullness of God.
>
> Ephesians 3:16–19

Rebuilding our emotional lives will deepen our spirituality and take our relationship with God to levels we have never known before. There are six simple steps to get us moving on this journey to the next stage of our walk with God.

### 1. Emotional Vocabulary

> Gentle words are a tree of life; a deceitful tongue crushes the spirit.
>
> Proverbs 15:4, NLT

We cannot develop an emotional life without an emotional vocabulary. Far too few of us actually know enough words to communicate the emotions we feel on a regular basis. Developing an emotional vocabulary is one of the first things I recommend to teens and I would also recommend it to adults. Try downloading an emotions chart and familiarizing yourself with the terms. I consider myself fairly well versed in emotions but was humbled when I saw how many words there were for emotions I had never considered, but had definitely felt. As a starting point, you can use the small emotions chart included in the notes page at the end of this chapter.

**2. Emotional Awareness**

> And when a prayer or plea is made by anyone among your people Israel—being aware of their afflictions and pains, and spreading out their hands toward this temple— then hear from heaven, your dwelling place. Forgive, and deal with everyone according to all they do, since you know their hearts (for you alone know the human heart), so that they will fear you and walk in obedience to you all the time they live in the land you gave our ancestors.
>
> 2 Chronicles 6:29–31

Once we develop our emotional vocabulary, we will be able to increase our emotional awareness. We will have words to describe a number of feelings we have had, but have never known how to explain. We can learn from Solomon's prayer in the above scripture that increasing our emotional awareness will make our prayers much more intimate and influential with God. When we are aware of our afflictions and pains and take them to God, he hears us and takes action. Another valuable benefit is that it will increase the depth and intimacy of our human relationships.

### 3. Emotional History

*One who has unreliable friends soon comes to ruin, but there is a friend who sticks closer than a brother.*

Proverbs 18:24

Once we have increased our emotional vocabulary and awareness, we will experience immediate benefits in our relationships with God and people. After experiencing these initial benefits, it is wise to develop an emotional history. What is an emotional history and how do we put one together? It's quite simple: We begin by looking back over our lives and reflecting on our significant relationships. Then we look for patterns by asking a few basic questions:

1. Which of my relationships have had the most significant emotional impact on my life? How did these relationships begin? How did they end? If I am still close to these people, what are the qualities that have allowed these relationships to endure?
2. Which relationships in my life have ended badly and why?
3. What are the best relationships in my life, and what are the qualities that have kept them strong and healthy?

Once we have developed an emotional history of our lives, we should communicate the lessons learned to our closest friends. When we have difficulty in our relationships, we should review our history. We can then take responsibility if we are repeating unhealthy patterns and strive to apply our strengths to improve our relationships.

### 4. Emotional Honesty

> Lord, who may dwell in your sacred tent? Who may live on your holy mountain? The one whose walk is blameless, who does what is righteous, who speaks the truth from their heart.
>
> Psalm 15:1–2

Regardless of how much introspection or reflection we do, nothing matters more to our spiritual and emotional lives than honesty—speaking the truth from our hearts. Rebuilding our emotional life demands honesty, which means we must make a decision not to disguise our true feelings with our lips.

> Enemies <u>disguise themselves with their lips</u>, but in their hearts they harbor deceit.
>
> Proverbs 26:24

We must make repeated decisions to open up about the reality of our lives, which includes being honest and vulnerable about our guilt and sins with ourselves, with God, and with our friends.

> I have a message from God in my heart concerning the sinfulness of the wicked: There is no fear of God before their eyes. In their own eyes they flatter themselves too much to detect or hate their sin.
>
> Psalm 36:1–2

This honesty is not something we simply practice on the outside, because all true honesty begins on the inside. We must be willing to tell ourselves the truth.

> But you desire honesty from the womb, teaching me wisdom even there.
>
> Psalm 51:6, NLT

This type of truth-telling is difficult to do on our own, which is why the Bible encourages us to build spiritual relationships that include the practice of emotional honesty.

> See to it, brothers and sisters, that none of you has a sinful, unbelieving heart that turns away from the living God. But encourage one another daily, as long as it is called "Today," so that none of you may be hardened by sin's deceitfulness.
>
> Hebrews 3:12–13

There is no more important quality for rebuilding our emotional lives than emotional honesty. We need to rely on God and begin practicing it today.

### 5. Emotional Maturity

> We have much to say about this, but it is hard to make it clear to you because you no longer try to understand. In fact, though by this time you ought to be teachers, you need someone to teach you the elementary truths of God's word all over again. You need milk, not solid food! Anyone who lives on milk, being still an infant, is not acquainted with the teaching about righteousness. But solid food is for the mature, who by constant use have trained themselves to distinguish good from evil.
>
> Hebrews 5:11–14

Emotional maturity is a balanced and resilient temperament that allows us to make connections with all types of people. When we walk with God through all that life throws at us, we inevitably develop emotional maturity—we learn how to process and manage our emotions in a healthy and effective way. Emotional maturity has very little to do with age and everything to do with consistency. To become emotionally mature, we have to work on it every day and in every relationship. It is an absolute necessity if we hope to teach others to walk with God, build healthy relationships, and make a positive contribution in this world. Parents, teachers, coaches, corporate and political leaders—really all people of influence—must have emotional maturity to help and inspire others.

### 6. Emotional Connections

> But in fact God has placed the parts in the body, every one of them, just as he wanted them to be. If they were all one part, where would the body be? As it is, there are many parts, but one body. The eye cannot say to the hand, "I don't need you!" And the head cannot say to the feet, "I don't need you!"
>
> 1 Corinthians 12:18–21

The sixth and final step in emotional rebuilding is the acceptance that we are different from everyone else. One of the great joys in life should be making emotional connections with others who are equally unique. Making emotional connections is a messy business, and we all have a number of emotional challenges to deal with. Every family, group, or organization of which we are a part will be messy. This includes the church. As

Christians, we must have the type of patient and deep love that allows us to make intimate and loyal emotional connections. This is what will make both our God and his church attractive.

In our next chapter, we will discuss and develop a game plan we can implement that will make God attractive to ourselves and others. Read on and let's be inspired together.

**CHAPTER SIX: HOW GOD BECOMES SATISFYING**

# DIVE DEEP: Pause and Reflect
Jot down notes you want to remember from each section

### 6.1 HOW GOD BECOMES SATISFYING
Rebuilding our emotional lives

Emotional Inventory
Numbers 33:1-2

1.) Emotionally Defensive
Ruth 1:12-13, 14-18

2.) Emotionally Detached
Luke 5:8, 10

3.) Emotionally Immature
Judges 6:15, 16

4.) Emotionally Insecure
2 Samuel 6:9, Psalm 30:2-6

5.) Emotionally Numb
Isaiah 26:16, Jeremiah 20:7, Jeremiah 20:9

6.) Emotional Rebuilding
Luke 6:47-49, Ephesisans 3:16-19

What are your strengths and your weaknesses?

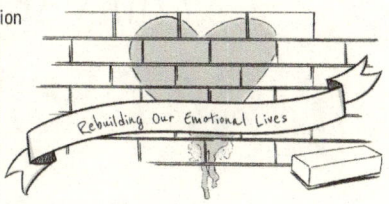

### 6.2 THE 6 SIMPLE STEPS TO START THE NEXT STAGE OF OUR WALK WITH GOD

1.) Emotional Vocabulary
Proverbs 25:11

2.) Emotional Awareness
2 Chronicles 6:29-31

3.) Emotional History
Proverbs 18:24

4.) Emotional Honesty
Psalm 15:1-2, Proverbs 26:24, Psalm 36:1-2, Psalm 51:6, Hebrews 3:12-13

5.) Emotional Maturity
Hebrews 5:11-14

6. Emotional Connections
1 Corinthians 12:18-21

1 BIG TAKEAWAY:

Scan this QR code with your phone's camera to check out the latest resources on this chapter here

# CHAPTER SEVEN:
# WHAT MAKES GOD ATTRACTIVE

*How We Can Change the World*

Blessed are the pure in heart, <u>for they will see God</u>.

Matthew 5:8

There is a dream that lives in the heart of every man and woman who believes in the goodness and greatness of God. It is a dream of a world left better for our having been here—a world transformed by the love, power, and truth of our great God.

Every day I see this dream coming true in individual lives. Just the other day I was talking to a young man named Gary, who was visiting our church. Gary said to me, "You are responsible for me being here." Since I had only just met him, I was somewhat confused by the statement.

Before I could ask a question he said, "A friend of mine told me I should attend your church, and so I decided to visit. The day I came, you preached a sermon about God being a spiritual father and the difficulty we would experience in our relationship with him if we had a negative view of our physical father. I cried through that entire sermon because all my adult life I have wanted to kill my father."

I was totally captivated and intrigued by Gary's story. Then he went on to say, "I jumped on a plane to visit my father who lives overseas. I was praying that I would have a change of heart toward him. I had a copy of the sermon with me when I went to see him. I told him everything was good between us, and he needed to listen to the sermon. It was amazing. I couldn't believe God had changed me."

When he finished this story, I was reminded of how important it is to keep our focus on God. I thought of how easy it is to replace God with religion, people, or even emotion, and that none of these things can produce this kind of change. This is the kind of change that makes God attractive. Inspiring ourselves as well as others to see God's attractiveness will change the world.

## CHANGING THE WORLD

> From him the whole body, joined and held together by every supporting ligament, grows and builds itself up in love, <u>as each part does its work</u>.
>
> Ephesians 4:16

What I failed to tell you about Gary was that my sermon was only one of several things that had changed his life. It wasn't even the most important contribution. His life change was a result of the collective efforts described in Ephesians 4:16.

While Gary and I were talking, Jim, a member of our church, was standing next to him. Jim was Gary's friend, co-worker, and one of the people who had been involved in Gary's emotional journey toward reconciliation with his father. God used Jim, as well as a number of other people, to change Gary's life. Their individual relationships with God were so attractive, they inspired Gary to develop his own.

Why is all of this important? Sermons preached in church services can't change this world. The world is changed when one person's relationship with God is so attractive, it inspires others to seek him, too. This is something I have grown to appreciate over the last decade. I have worked with my team to infuse this mindset into our church culture, encouraging each individual to develop their own personal walk with God that makes him attractive to others, much like the church of the New Testament.

The church we read about in the New Testament was not made strong by the celebrity of an individual superstar preacher. It was made strong by the powerful walk with God of each individual Christian. The collective power of these individual walks with God made the early church a transformative force in the world.

This transformative church can live again, but we will need a new kind of faith to restore what is essentially, in our time, a new kind of church. This means thinking and building differently than we have in the past. It requires making a paradigm shift in how we live, lead, and build in our churches.

## PARADIGM SHIFT

> I often point out that if an American were put in a time capsule in 1895 and it was opened 100 years later, there would be few things in American life that person would recognize; transportation, communications, and virtually every facet of daily life would have changed. The only American enterprise with which our latter-day Rip Van

## CHAPTER SEVEN: WHAT MAKES GOD ATTRACTIVE

Winkle would be comfortable is our schools, since they are remarkably similar to the schools we had before the Spanish American War.

—Louis V. Gerstner[14]

The problem with some of our churches is one similar to that of our schools—they are stuck in the nineteenth century, strangely frozen in time. This becomes evident whenever the word "change" is mentioned on their hallowed grounds. Committees meet to discuss the theological arguments for or against change. Camps form on either side of the issue, threats are made, sometimes people are fired, and the church splits. About ten years later, we do it again. Despite all this activity, our churches remain largely the same. This pattern of implosion has been going on for decades, if not centuries.

How do we end this counterproductive and repetitive cycle? How can we create churches that are God-centered spiritual communities, where people are more interested in making God attractive than in getting their own way? I believe the answer to these questions begins with a willingness to innovate. While not deviating from biblical truths, we need to develop innovative church cultures where every believer welcomes innovative thought, innovative action, and the changes they produce. This includes practical and useful ideas that come from people who have no interest in God or the church.

We need to get outside the "bubble" of our church and find out what is going on in the rest of the world. What do they know that we don't know, and how can we use this knowledge to build lives and churches that make God attractive? This type of thinking led to the creation of one of the most innovative and flexible churches in the entire New Testament.

> Now those who had been scattered by the persecution that broke out when Stephen was killed traveled as far as Phoenicia, Cyprus and Antioch, <u>spreading the word only among Jews</u>. Some of them, however, men from Cyprus and Cyrene, went to Antioch and <u>began to speak to Greeks also</u>, telling them the good news about the Lord Jesus. The Lord's hand was with them, and a great number of people believed and turned to the Lord.
>
> Acts 11:19–21

This groundbreaking church was located in the largely Gentile (i.e., non-Jewish, and often non-religious) city of Antioch. The church was started by some cutting-edge Christians who decided to also speak to the Greeks rather than limit the message of Jesus to the Jews only. This created a paradigm shift that reverberated throughout the entire Christian community for years.

"Paradigm shift" is a phrase popularized by business thinker and writer Joel Barker, who believes that all organizations are governed by a set of rules, patterns, and boundaries that he calls paradigms. While paradigms help us to get things done, they can also limit our vision and cause us to resist change. Barker calls it a paradigm shift when these rules, patterns, or boundaries change.

The disciples of Jesus in Antioch began inspiring Gentiles to seek God and become disciples, but this was at odds with the rules, patterns, and boundaries of the then largely Jewish church. The established powers of the church were located in Jerusalem and were just beginning to digest Peter's message that Gentiles should be welcomed into the church too.

**CHAPTER SEVEN: WHAT MAKES GOD ATTRACTIVE**

While the Jewish majority was slowly adjusting to change, the Antioch church was being used by God to create a paradigm shift. Its rapid growth increased the numbers of Gentile believers. Suddenly, the cultural lock Judaism had on the church began to give way to a rising tide of Gentile thought. In fact, as Gentiles became more familiar with this new faith, they gave its believers a new name—"Christian"—and as the years went by, the old name— "disciple" —became obsolete.

The disciples were called Christians <u>first at Antioch</u>.

Acts 11:26

This name change foreshadowed the reality that, in time, the Gentiles would grow to become a greater influence on the church than the Jews. Just as the word "disciple" would fade from use, so would the influence of the Jews on the church as God's message rang out to the larger global audience of the world—the Gentiles. For years, the Jewish Christians would fight for relevance, but they would learn—as we all must—that a paradigm shift is a powerful force. Once unleashed, a paradigm shift is difficult, if not impossible, to stop—especially when God is behind it.

Paradigm shifts, like the one experienced by the New Testament Christians, keep our faith, fellowship, and churches vibrant. This vibrancy makes God attractive. My belief is that with a flexible and innovative faith like the faith of the Christians in Antioch, we can break free from the past, reimagine the church, and make God attractive in this twenty-first century.

## LEADERSHIP THAT LASTS

> No one will thank you for taking care of the present if you have neglected the future.
>
> —Joel Barker[15]

Paradigm shifts call for decisions to live by faith rather than letting ourselves be limited by traditions, rules, or denominational cultures. We need to reimagine our relationship with God, each other, and the church. This means that we have to change the way we think. We have to let go of old assumptions about God and dead ideas about religion. We have to look at the Bible with fresh eyes, a renewed desire to obey, a hunger to learn how the world can be inspired, and what will make God attractive.

I still remember the paradigm shift that forced me to admit my thinking about God and his church was limited, dull, and lacked the spirit of innovation necessary to produce an inspiring church, like the one in Antioch. Gail and I had just moved our family to the Bay Area. The technology and Internet revolution of the 1990s was in its early stages. I had the good fortune of taking part in a workshop on innovation that included the cutting-edge business and organizational thinker, Jim Collins. He was releasing his first best-seller called *Built to Last* on the same day I heard him teach.

Through his teaching and his answers to very specific questions I had asked about the organizational behavior of my church, I learned that we were what Collins calls "time tellers," who needed to become "clock builders."[16] Time teller organizations are essentially dependent on one great idea or charismatic leader. This leader tells everyone in the

## CHAPTER SEVEN: WHAT MAKES GOD ATTRACTIVE

organization the time. Clock builder organizations are built to prosper far beyond the life of any single idea or leader. They build clocks so that everyone in the organization can tell the time.

The first thing I did was accept that I was a time teller. The second thing I did was decide to become a clock builder. I began talking with my wife, Gail, as well as my closest spiritual friends about our leadership philosophy. We consulted with people both inside and outside the church who understood how to build healthy and effective organizations. We also started to read the Bible differently.

As a result, a whole new world opened up to us. We have had the opportunity to make some transformative changes in the way we think, lead, and build. We are more focused on God and less focused on people. This has created a refreshingly unified and creative church culture that enthusiastically embraces change. This culture has made it easier to invest in our youth. Those who are older are much more committed to building a great future than holding on to an obsolete past. Having our eyes focused on the future has helped us realize that our church must be more than a fad; we are building a Bay Area institution. This is why we have made it a priority to invest in our local communities and the metropolitan area as a whole.

Together with the Christians in our church, we are on a quest to build a spiritual community like the one that existed in Antioch, where believers understood, learned from, and inspired the secular community of which they were a part. The dream God has laid on our hearts is to build a church that makes him attractive to the world around us for generations to come. We recognize that this task is enormous. It is beyond the skill or ability of any man, woman, or organization but well within the capability of our great God. We have a long way to go, but we recognize that what we are building together is more important than what any of us could do on our own.

This is why we are working hard to make sure every Christian experiences the power of a transformational relationship with God. This alone will fulfill our dream of a church that makes God attractive, a dream I hope and pray others will believe can also happen for them.

## SOMETHING TO BELIEVE IN

> Great is the Lord and most worthy of praise; <u>his greatness no one can fathom</u>.
>
> Psalm 145:3

This dream will not be possible unless we stem the spiritual decline going on in many of our churches. A spiritual decline in churches and individuals is almost always rooted in a failure of faith. To create a paradigm shift that will produce transformational change, we have to do more than make organizational adjustments. People lose faith in God and turn away from him because they no longer find him, or anything related to him, attractive.

We must find a way to make him attractive to those who do not currently find him so. This means we must focus more on him and less on ourselves. We will have to let go of some traditions, ideas, and opinions we have held dear. We will have to be flexible, innovative, and open to change. We have to find a way to help people see the greatness of God so that they can find the faith to believe again.

> What is more, I consider everything a loss because of the surpassing worth of knowing Christ Jesus my Lord, for whose sake I have lost all things. I consider them garbage, that I may gain Christ.
>
> Philippians 3:8

When we see God accurately through the life of Jesus Christ, we become more and more aware of his greatness. In contrast, when we try to change him to fit our expectations and desires, we create him in our own image, and he ceases to be great.

> You can safely assume that you've created God in your own image when it turns out that God hates all the same people you do.
>
> –Anne Lamott[17]

People speak and write about all the evil done in the name of religion, but fail to see, investigate, or report that, in almost every tragedy related to modern-day religion, the perpetrators failed to believe in or reflect the truth about God. This is not a new problem; it is consistently addressed in Scripture in passages like Jeremiah 7:30–31, which points out that the people of God were doing things in his name that had never entered his mind.

> The people of Judah have done evil in my eyes, declares the Lord. They have set up their detestable idols in the house that bears my Name and have defiled it. They have built the high places of Topheth in the Valley of Ben Hinnom to burn their sons and daughters in the fire— something I did not command, <u>nor did it enter my mind</u>.
>
> Jeremiah 7:30–31

Throughout Scripture and secular recorded history, evil done in God's name has not, in fact, originated with him. It typically originated with someone whose view of God was inaccurate and far less than great. In Scripture, the men and women who did great things always had or developed a view of God that reflected his greatness. Nehemiah was just such a man. He was chosen by God to do great things and he possessed an accurate view of God as great.

> Then I said: "Lord, the God of heaven, the great and awesome God, who keeps his covenant of love with those who love him and keep his commandments, let your ear be attentive and your eyes open to hear the prayer your servant is praying before you day and night for your servants, the people of Israel. I confess the sins we Israelites, including myself and my father's family, have committed against you.
>
> Nehemiah 1:5-6

When studying the life of Nehemiah, we discover that our personal view of God is more important than the level of our talent or our ability to do the job. Nehemiah certainly believed this. He consistently chose to direct people's attention to God's power rather than to his own leadership.

> After I looked things over, I stood up and said to the nobles, the officials and the rest of the people, "<u>Don't be afraid</u> of them. <u>Remember the Lord</u>, who is great and awesome, and fight for your families, your sons and your daughters, your wives and your homes."
>
> Nehemiah 4:14

Nehemiah was very different from Samson, who was another one of God's leaders. Samson's story can be found in Judges 13-16. Samson possessed great talent and ability. He dominated wherever he went. He was very much a time teller in the way that he led the people of Israel. The people were focused on Samson as a leader and not focused on God. He could not rally a nation because his small and inadequate view of God did not allow him empower others to build their own personal faith in God.

On the other hand, Nehemiah lacked the natural talent of Samson, but he was able to rally a nation to rebuild. His confidence in, and dependence upon, God was obvious in his prayer, recorded in Nehemiah 9:32:

> Now therefore, our God, the great God, mighty and awesome, who keeps his covenant of love, do not let all this hardship seem trifling in your eyes—the hardship that has come on us, on our kings and leaders, on our priests and prophets, on our ancestors and all your people, from the days of the kings of Assyria until today.

Nehemiah's view of God and relationship with him inspired the people. He passed that faith on to the men and women of Israel. This faith in God inspired them to build a wall in the face of stiff opposition and revive the city of Jerusalem. Their success made it clear that their great God was alive, relevant, and attractive.

> So the wall was completed on the twenty-fifth of Elul, in fifty-two days. When all our enemies heard about this, all the surrounding nations were <u>afraid and lost their self-confidence</u>, because they realized that this work had been done <u>with the help of our God</u>.
>
> Nehemiah 6:15–16

The men and women who will influence, shape, and change this world must possess a view of God that recognizes his greatness. Religion in general, and Christianity in particular, fails when we see God as less than great.

## TALK IS CHEAP

All hard work brings a profit, but <u>mere talk leads only to poverty</u>.

Proverbs 14:23

Scan to listen to a music playlist on this topic.

My grandmother was a religious person, so I am fairly certain that, if she were alive today, she would have read this book. I am equally certain that she would have been open to the idea that her view of God needed to change and rise to the level of someone like Nehemiah. At some point, she would have said what she often told me when my mouth made claims my life couldn't back up: "Russell, talk is cheap." My grandmother was never one for talk. She judged me by my actions, not my claims.

The same principle holds true for making God attractive. People who are seeking God will judge us by our actions, not our claims. Therefore, we must be very careful. We are likely to applaud the idea of developing an accurate view of God, especially a view rooted in God's greatness. In fact, we may be tempted to hold seminars, workshops, and small groups built around the idea of changing our view of God. While more teaching and discussion is admirable, there is an important lesson to be learned from Nehemiah's life: the person who truly sees God as great will let his or her actions do the talking.

Changing our view of God is not a passive decision, but an inspired one. When we begin to understand, know, and draw close to God, mere talk will not satisfy us. God will keep our lamp of inspiration burning and we will want to do something great with our lives.

> You, LORD, keep my lamp burning; my God turns my darkness into light. With your help I can advance against a troop; with my God I can scale a wall.
>
> Psalm 18:28–29

This was true of Nehemiah, whose relationship with God allowed the lamp of his heart to burn so brightly, he was able to see God's vision for his life. In fact, he carried this dream with sadness until it could be fulfilled.

> In the month of Nisan in the twentieth year of King Artaxerxes, when wine was brought for him, I took the wine and gave it to the king. I had not been sad in his presence before, so the king asked me, "Why does your face look so sad when you are not ill? This can be nothing but sadness of heart." I was very much afraid, but I said to the king, "May the king live forever! Why should my face not look sad when the city where my fathers are buried lies in ruins, and its gates have been destroyed by fire?"
>
> Nehemiah 2:1–3

Once the king gave him permission to take action on the dream, Nehemiah carried it in his heart to Jerusalem, with God as his only partner. This cemented their intimacy, and Nehemiah gained a confidence that was unshakable in the face of even the fiercest opposition.

> I went to Jerusalem, and after staying there three days I set out during the night with a few others. <u>I had not told anyone what my God had put in my heart to do for Jerusalem.</u> There were no mounts with me except the one I was riding on.
>
> Nehemiah 2:11–12

## CHAPTER SEVEN: WHAT MAKES GOD ATTRACTIVE

Nehemiah's intimacy with God gave him the confidence to take action and inspired others to join him.

> Then I said to them, "You see the trouble we are in: Jerusalem lies in ruins, and its gates have been burned with fire. <u>Come, let us rebuild the wall of Jerusalem</u>, and we will no longer be in disgrace." I also told them about <u>the gracious hand of my God on me</u> and what the king had said to me. <u>They replied, "Let us start rebuilding."</u> So they began this good work.
>
> Nehemiah 2:17–18

Once they took action, they met repeated opposition at various stages of the rebuilding, but because of his relationship with God, Nehemiah's confidence was unshakable.

> But when Sanballat the Horonite, Tobiah the Ammonite official and Geshem the Arab heard about it, <u>they mocked and ridiculed us</u>. "What is this you are doing?" they asked. "Are you rebelling against the king?" <u>I answered them</u> by saying, "<u>The God of heaven will give us success</u>. We his servants will start rebuilding, but as for you, you have no share in Jerusalem or any claim or historic right to it."
>
> Nehemiah 2:19–20

Nehemiah was willing to take such bold action because he did not merely agree intellectually that God was great—he really believed it. This is exactly the type of active faith that God desires today from those who believe in him. God knows that theories, platitudes, and religious behaviors cannot inspire those who find him unattractive. They need to see

Christians living lives of action and changing the world right before their eyes.

Nehemiah's inspiration should be our own. We should see God as great and then look at, listen to, and believe in the dreams he puts on our hearts. No matter how small or big the dream, we should trust God and pursue it. This is how he leads us to make a difference—and that makes him attractive.

I can still remember the first time God put an idea on my heart. It happened just a few years after I had decided to make the ministry my career of choice and forget about politics. I had returned from school in Boston to spend the Christmas holiday with my family in my hometown of Kentwood, Michigan.

During the time I was in Kentwood, I attended a local church in downtown Grand Rapids that served as my spiritual home. As luck would have it, the usual speaker was taking a break, and in his place was a visiting speaker with whom I had an indirect relationship connection. I can't remember which of us initiated getting together, but somehow we set up an appointment after church.

He and his wife were a seasoned and experienced ministry couple whose background was somewhat different from the ministers who were mentoring me back in Boston. I decided to take advantage of this opportunity to ask questions and learn. That evening was educational in a number of ways, but the most stirring subject was when we discussed the differences between the Black and white branches of our particular fellowship of churches.

In their minds, the Black and white branches of the church would never come together as one. They said, "It will never happen." They went on to say, "Churches will never reach the point where they will be racially mixed. That's just the way the world is and there is nothing you can do to change that."

At first, I was stunned that someone who believed in God would have such a pessimistic and fatalistic view of the future. Then it dawned on me that the church I was attending in Boston was primarily white and the one in Grand Rapids was primarily African American. I recalled that I had never seen or attended a truly diverse church. The facts supported their position, but something made me open my mouth and say, "If that is the way the world is, then I want to change the world."

This minister's sober truth telling disturbed me because he was telling me that my spiritual life was going to be just like my previous secular life. He was telling me that the things I had found insurmountable before I had a relationship with God would remain insurmountable, though now I had a relationship with God. He was telling me to believe that a relationship with God didn't really make a difference in this world. To me, this was the same thing as saying that God was good and well-meaning, but absolutely not great.

I suppose there was a bit of naïve arrogance involved in my statement that I wanted to change the world. After all, I was all of twenty-one years old and hadn't even mastered simple things like paying my phone bill. Nevertheless, a dream was born. I decided then and there to adopt the mindset of Robert Kennedy to "dream of things that never were" and say, "Why not?"[18]

After I returned to Boston, I slowly began to connect the dots. I realized that my evening with that minister was not the first time I had come face-to-face with this pessimistic and fatalistic worldview. Throughout my life, Black people had told me that you couldn't trust white people. And white people, through their actions more than their words, showed me that they didn't trust Black people.

I didn't agree with either assessment and decided that, rather than accept the world as they saw it, I would rely on God to shape a world based on his power rather than the pessimism of man. This would be a world where Black and white people would not merely become legally tolerant of each other, but would actually accept each other and build healthy relationships in their communities.

This dream was planted in my heart, and I am grateful today to be a part of the Bay Area Christian Church, where our diversity is something that only God could have accomplished. Sitting, loving, and laughing together on a weekly basis is that "rainbow coalition" that Reverend Jesse Jackson has referred to on so many occasions. It's not as a country coerced by law, but as brothers and sisters bound together by the powerful blood of Jesus—the blood that makes us family.

> Our flag is red, white and blue, but our nation is a rainbow-red, yellow, brown, black and white—and we're all precious in God's sight.
>
> —Jesse Jackson[19]

Since those early days and my conversation with that well-intentioned minister, I have learned that when we see people limiting God to merely the good, we must strive for the great. We must "dream of things that never were," and say, "Why not?" We must make a difference, because this is what makes God attractive.

## IS THIS OUR TIME?

> By calling this covenant "new," he has made the first one obsolete; and what is obsolete and outdated will soon disappear.
>
> Hebrews 8:13

When I look back on my conversation with that minister from the perspective of added age and experience, I understand him better. He had almost certainly fought and won some difficult battles. When he looked at himself, his family, and his church, he saw great progress and success. I am sure he saw the limitations as well, and realized that there comes a time when a person has to stop dreaming about tomorrow and be satisfied with today.

Today I can feel that same temptation. There are days when loosening my grip on the idealism of my youth seems wise. Why not celebrate how far we have come rather than reach for more? Why not be satisfied with a few dreams coming true rather than listening for more? Why not leave well enough alone?

I have reflected on all this and come to one clear conclusion: when the dream no longer stirs us, when fatigue prompts us to settle, when miracles no longer seem possible—something needs to change! It is time to question not the dream, but what we are doing.

When God saw the old covenant failing, he let it die. We should learn from him. When we see that what we are doing is failing, we should let it die. This is what I believe that minister from long ago could not do—he could not bring himself to believe in his God more than in his church. It didn't occur to him that if his church said something great was not possible, it was the church that needed to change, not the dream.

His view of God was not great enough for him to believe the church could change. Now, as I age, I realize the same question has come to me. When God lays on my heart a dream too big for the human church, do I change my view of God or do I change the church?

Here in the twenty-first century, I believe this is a question each of us must ask. We are living in a country and a world that has lost its grip on hope and grows more weary every day. Every day and everywhere, pessimism, fatalism, defeatism, and cynicism rear their ugly heads. Hopelessness abounds as people settle for survival, accept decline as inevitable, and pack their dreams away in storage, along with all the rest of hope's memorabilia.

If ever there was a time for the greatness of God to be seen, known, and exemplified in the lives of those who know him, this would be it. Do we have a view of God that is great enough to bring hope to a hopeless world? Do we belong to churches whose members share a collective view of God that is great enough to make a difference in this world? Do we understand that it is in the dark and discouraging times of despair that the greatness of God can most easily be seen? Have we considered that the times we live in cry out for us to act and make God attractive to our generation?

## MAKING GOD ATTRACTIVE

> Change is the law of life. And those who look only to the past or present are certain to miss the future.
>
> —John F. Kennedy[20]

## CHAPTER SEVEN: WHAT MAKES GOD ATTRACTIVE

Our church has been working to embrace innovation as a core conviction because we believe that the problems we are facing today cannot be solved with yesterday's thinking. We don't want to become the old church on the side of the road of progress. We don't want to block the way of the next innovative thinker, who questions assumptions we have taken as gospel truth. For this reason, we have come to believe that the only way to continue making a positive impact on the world is by allowing some of our old religious ways and thoughts to die so that new ones can be born and live.

Seeing God as great means seeing life in relation to him and the possibilities he can bring to pass. It means embracing idealism, hope, and vision. Those who choose this life will dream. They will look to the future with a faith capable of both seeing and creating new opportunities to make God attractive. They will be Christians who change the world. The message of God's attractiveness will ring out from their lives.

> And so <u>you became</u> a model to all the believers in Macedonia and Achaia. The Lord's <u>message rang out from you</u> not only in Macedonia and Achaia—<u>your faith in God has become known everywhere</u>. Therefore we <u>do not need to say anything about it</u>.
>
> 1 Thessalonians 1:7–8

What dream has God placed on your heart? What dream is supposed to bring you and God closer together? What dreams has he placed on the hearts of those in your church?

Each one of us has something in our lives that God can and wants to use to make himself attractive. Perhaps it is something you love, but others fail to appreciate. Maybe it is a chronic illness, personal tragedy, disability, or terrible loss that God wants to help you overcome, so you can inspire those in similar circumstances. Sometimes it is a unique talent that you have kept hidden or buried out of insecurity. It might even be an impossible dream that, if mentioned aloud, would cause others to laugh. We need to overcome the fear and doubt that have kept us paralyzed for too long and believe that, with God, our lives can and will make a difference.

Sometimes we have to look to those who have gone before us to understand and be reminded that each of us can make a difference. My reminder came when Eunice Shriver died in 2009. Eunice Shriver had a sister named Rose, to whom she was very close. Her love for and experience with Rose inspired her to create the Special Olympics. Eunice made a difference so profound that some consider her the most important Kennedy. *US News & World Report* said in its cover story on November 15, 1993, "When the full judgment of the Kennedy legacy is made—including JFK's Peace Corps and Alliance for Progress, Robert Kennedy's passion for civil rights and Ted Kennedy's efforts on health care, workplace reform, and refugees—the changes wrought by Eunice Shriver may well be seen as the most consequential."[21]

In 2007, Edward Kennedy stated that his sister Eunice was an agent of change. "If the test is what you're doing that's been helpful for humanity, you'd be hard-pressed to find another member of the family who's done more."[22]

Eunice Shriver's love and passion for people with special needs ran strong, as is evidenced by her 1987 speech at the Special Olympic World Games in South Bend, Indiana where she said, "You are the stars and the world is watching you. By your presence, you send a message to every village, every city, every nation. A message of hope. A message of victory."[23]

As a parent of children with special needs, it is incredibly inspiring to hear words that give dignity to the special-needs community and to all who have disabilities. In the same speech, she went on to talk about the rights that these children and adults had earned by their efforts:

> *The right to play on any playing field?*
> *You have earned it.*
> *The right to study in any school?*
> *You have earned it.*
> *The right to hold a job?*
> *You have earned it.*
> *The right to be anyone's neighbor?*
> *You have earned it.*[24]

Perhaps what is most stirring about her life is the impact she had on her children, one of whom is Tim Shriver, the current head of Special Olympics. He was interviewed by the NPR "Online News Hour" on July 12, 2006. Mr. Shriver described growing up with a mother who wanted to make a difference by serving others.

> Well, if you look at her camps—you know, I was a child in the '60s. I was born in 1959. But I remember very clearly—I don't know exactly what age, whether it was five or six years old—I remember looking out my window in the morning and seeing people come from institutions, get off yellow school buses, empty out into my backyard, raise the American flag, sing songs, and then fan out for kickball, or for swimming, or for horseback riding in this beautiful Maryland farm.[25]

He described the influence of his mother's service on his own life:

> It took me a long time to realize that that wasn't normal. You know, to have a hundred or so young people with intellectual disabilities in your backyard wasn't a normal summer activity. But she was doing that because she went to those places and she saw the fetid institutions. She saw the neglect. She saw people sitting there, and she knew they were young people.[26]

Approximately two weeks after Eunice Shriver died, her younger brother Ted died, as well. Eunice's father had said that if she had been born a boy, she would have been the one who became president.

*Meet the Press* dedicated an entire show to the death of Ted Kennedy, with a central portion of the telecast including an interview with Eunice's daughter, Maria Shriver. There were many compelling things in the interview with Maria Shriver, but one stands out. She spoke about the fact that both her mother and her uncle dedicated their lives to a cause—her mother to individuals with disabilities and Ted to getting proper health care for every American.

Maria Shriver said that in this world speed is everything, and few people can make the type of difference her mother and uncle made because they are unwilling to devote their lives to a cause. But, she kept repeating, this type of dedication is the only way the world can be changed.[27]

I reflected on this during the celebration of the lives of these two Kennedys and began to realize that my paradigm for making God attractive needed to change. It wasn't sufficient to keep trotting out tried and true traditional ways of making him attractive. I had to search for, invent, and innovate to meet the needs of the people around me, if I was going to make God attractive to them.

During that time, I reflected on the things our church had done for the community to help families and individuals with special needs. One of these programs was E-Soccer, with the "E" standing for how anyone can be "exceptional." It started because I wanted to allow my kids, who have special needs, to participate in sports with kids who were neurotypical (those without special needs). I was fortunate enough to have some good friends with soccer backgrounds as well as families with neurotypical kids who wanted to help out.

We started out in a field where we often had to clean up after a flock of Canadian geese before we could get started, but nothing could stop our ambitious little group from making this small dream come true. We were determined to practice inclusion, which meant that the kids with special needs were involved with the typical kids in everything. Typical kids were partnered with those with special needs, and under the guidance of the coaches, every kid began to make progress in numerous areas of their lives.

Eventually, people from the neighborhood and community found out about it and wanted to join in. That one little idea has now grown into more than twenty programs serving thousands of people all over the Bay Area. The inclusive spirit of E-Soccer inspired some of our volunteers to start their own E-programs in other sports like basketball (E-Hoops), dance, karate, and fitness. More recently, E-Sports expanded into an umbrella program called E-Life, with pilot programs in E-Gardening, E-Photography, and E-Studying already underway.

The impact E-Soccer had on the community became so notable that in 2007 I received the Jefferson Award because of my work with E-Soccer. Not long after that, former Congressman Tom Lantos honored me with a congressional citation because of my work with the program. We then launched the program in locations around the world and developed strong community partnerships with our local Major League Soccer team, the San Jose Earthquakes, and our NBA team, the Golden State Warriors.

I was shocked by the recognition and impact of E-Sports, because my original idea was simply to do something fun for my kids. That idea has turned into a community of families and volunteers whose shared interest is the joy and well-being of the kids and adults in the program. We are very proud of the fact that we have created this support network for families without any religious ties whatsoever. Our dream is that anyone and everyone can benefit from the acceptance and inclusion of E-Sports. That dream is coming true every day all over the Bay Area and in many other places around the world. You can learn more about E-Life and its many programs at e-life.org.

What I have learned from all of this is that sometimes we simply need to do good—not only as a church, but as individuals with our friends in the community. People don't have to join us for a church service; they don't even need to believe in God. We simply want to be the kind of people who, when others think of us, produce one central thought in their minds—those people sure make their God attractive.

In our final chapter, I want to encourage you to dig deep and turn your relationship with God into something more than

Bible reading and prayer. I will share some practical steps you can take to revive, rebuild, and redefine your relationship with God, so it stops being ordinary and becomes extraordinary.

If we make our pursuit of an extraordinary relationship with God our highest passion, it will have a transformative effect on our lives as well as on the lives of all with whom we have contact. We will be people blessed with God's inspiration and leadership. This will make us the kind of spiritual influence on this world that replaces hate with love, despair with hope, and cynicism with idealism. We will leave this world a better place for our children and our children's children. We will change the world.

# HE'S NOT WHO YOU THINK HE IS

## DIVE DEEP: Pause and Reflect
Jot down notes you want to remember from each section

**7.1 HOW WE CAN CHANGE THE WORLD**
Matthew 5:8

**7.2 CHANGING THE WORLD**
Ephesians 4:16

**7.3 PARADIGM SHIFT**
Acts 11:19-21, 26

**7.4 LEADERSHIP THAT LASTS**

**7.5 SOMETHING TO BELIEVE IN**
Psalm 145:3, Philippians 3:8, Jeremiah 7:30-31, Nehemiah 1:5-6, Nehemiah 4:14, Nehemiah 9:32, Nehemiah 6:15-16

**7.6 TALK IS CHEAP**
Proverbs 14:23, Psalm 18:28-29, Nehemiah 2:1-3, 11-12, 17-18, 19-20

Is This Our Time?
Hebrews 8:13

**7.7 MAKING GOD ATTRACTIVE**
1 Thessalonians 1:7-8

What dream has God placed on your heart?

What dream is supposed to bring you and God closer together?

What dreams has he placed on the hearts of those in your church?

1 BIG TAKEAWAY:

Scan this QR code with your phone's camera to check out the latest resources on this chapter here

152

## CHAPTER EIGHT:
# PRACTICAL STEPS FOR MAKING GOD ATTRACTIVE

*How to Develop Your Own Unique Relationship with God*

If there's a book you really want to read but it hasn't been written yet, then you must write it.

—Toni Morrison[28]

Before I became a Christian, I had no idea that Christian music, Christian books, or Christian bookstores existed. Even after I became a Christian and discovered these bookstores and products, my primary reason for visiting was to purchase a Bible. That all changed when I began to struggle spiritually. When I began to experience frustration, difficulty, and failure in my Christian life, I looked for books that would help me improve my relationship with God. What I discovered was that there weren't many writers dedicated to this subject. I found that odd because it seemed to me that God should be the obvious focus of Christianity.

One day, while wandering through a particularly large Christian bookstore in search of some inspiration about developing a relationship with God, I realized that every book on the subject was one I had either already read or had found inadequate for my needs. I was disappointed and realized that the kind of books I wanted to read were no longer being written. I think that was the day—many years ago now—that this book began.

My hope is that, by the grace of God, the ideas presented in this book have been thought-provoking, emotionally stirring, and inspirational. To make this book one that I myself would want to read, I've made this last section practical by including both information and guidance.

These are 20 steps that we can take to make God attractive and develop a unique relationship with him. What many would consider the foundational elements of a relationship with God (reading the Bible, praying, and attending a church) are included in this list. Each of these steps draws upon biblical sources for your continued study and reflection, and includes a QR code that will take you to a more in-depth devotional on the subject from Deep Spirituality. Any one of these steps, if deeply integrated into your heart, will help to transform your relationship with him.

1. Choose to know God.
2. Change your view of God.
3. Read to know God: Let Jesus teach you about him.
4. Pray so that God knows you.
5. Make it personal.

6. Tell God the truth.
7. See your sin, find forgiveness.
8. Feel some emotion.
9. Let God raise, train, and mature you.
10. Reflect and ask yourself questions.
11. Get to know yourself.
12. Identify your warning signs.
13. Increase your faith.
14. Think about God.
15. Talk about God.
16. Build healthy spiritual relationships.
17. Listen to learn what others know about God.
18. Use a different version of the Bible.
19. Use unconventional tools and methods.
20. Develop a transformational relationship with God.

## 1. CHOOSE TO KNOW GOD

*Reflect*

"I do not accept glory from human beings, but I know you. I know that you do not have the love of God in your hearts. I have come in my Father's name, and you do not accept me; but if someone else comes in his own name, you will accept him. How can you believe since you accept glory from one another but do not seek the glory that comes from the only God?"

John 5:41–44

Building relationships requires choice and effort. This is the point Jesus makes in John 5:41–44. He concludes that his listeners didn't love God because they failed to make the choice and were unwilling to make the effort to know him.

*Respond*

1. Which do you pursue with the greatest intensity: the praise of men or the praise of God?
2. What needs to change in your life so you can make knowing God a priority?
3. How can you increase your effort to build a relationship with God?

*Act*

Write down the names of three of your closest relationships. Reflect on how you decided to invest so much time and effort into these relationships. Make a decision to apply yourself in your relationship with God at least as much as you have with these three relationships.

## 2. CHANGE YOUR VIEW OF GOD

*Reflect*

"So I say to you: Ask and it will be given to you; seek and you will find; knock and the door will be opened to you. For everyone who asks receives; the one who seeks finds; and to the one who knocks, the door will be opened. Which of you fathers, if your son asks for a fish, will give him a snake instead? Or if he asks for an egg, will give him a scorpion? If you then, though you are evil, know how to give good gifts to your children, how much more will your Father in heaven give the Holy Spirit to those who ask him!"

Luke 11:9-13

The New Testament regularly refers to God as our father. On the face of it, this sounds good, but since there are no perfect father-child relationships, most people have difficulty understanding God as their father. In fact, any authority figure in our lives can influence our view of God as a father, and since none of them are perfect, we might have even more difficulty with this concept.

What does this mean? When we come to the Scriptures and see God as a father and authority, we will naturally attribute to him whatever thoughts and feelings we associate with those roles. For most people, the result is a combination of positive, negative, and misleading assumptions. Changing our view of God means keeping the positive, removing the negative, and correcting the misleading beliefs we hold.

*Respond*

1. What positive thoughts, feelings, or assumptions can you identify in your relationship with God?
2. What negative thoughts, feelings, or assumptions play a role in your relationship with God?
3. What misleading thoughts, feelings, or assumptions are influencing your relationship with God?

*Act*

If we are going to change our view of God, we have to develop a new and accurate vocabulary to describe him. One of the best ways to do this is to read the book of Psalms and circle every word that describes God. These words can help us develop a correct and accurate view of him.

## 3. READ TO KNOW GOD—LET JESUS TEACH YOU ABOUT HIM

### *Reflect*

> "You study the Scriptures diligently because you think that in them you have eternal life. These are the very Scriptures that testify about me, yet you refuse to come to me to have life."
>
> John 5:39–40

The mistake the religious people of Jesus' day made, and one we can also make, was to read the Scriptures as a rulebook or instruction manual. The religious Jews of Jesus' day were so busy developing their rules, arguments, and points of view that they completely missed the importance of relationship—they missed the value and importance of Jesus.

When we read the Bible, we should read it to know God. We can't allow ourselves to become so enamored by the characters, events, or arcane theological points that we miss the relationship. The Bible was written so we would know God, and only after knowing him can we truly understand the Scriptures.

### *Respond*

1. How have you been reading the Bible as a rulebook or instruction manual?
2. What can you do today to start reading the Bible to know God?

3. How can this change make reading the Bible more enjoyable?

*Act*

We live in an age of cynicism and negativity that affects our view of God. Often we can have a much more negative than positive view of him. One of the most effective things we can do to combat this problem is to read the Bible and circle the positive words that describe him. Then we should make a decision to believe what the Bible says about God and replace our negative thoughts with these positive ones.

## 4. PRAY WITH AN OPEN HEART

*Reflect*

> Search me, God, and know my heart; test me and know my anxious thoughts.
>
> Psalm 139:23

My wife, Gail, was the first person to open my eyes to the truth that praying with emotion establishes and increases our intimacy with God. Prior to receiving her help in this area, I rarely prayed with any emotion. Once I started to express how I felt when I prayed, my relationship with God was revolutionized. I felt closer to God, less burdened, less anxious, and far more secure. For the first time, I was being myself with God—I was allowing him to know me.

## Respond

1. How often do you express your emotions to God in prayer?
2. What emotions are you afraid to express to God? Why?
3. How can you increase your honesty with God so that he can know you better?

## Act

Communicating emotion and deep feeling in prayer requires solitude. It is difficult to pour our hearts out in the middle of a crowd or while others are watching. We need to make certain that we find solitary places where we can go from time to time to express our emotions to God and really allow him to know us. Find or make a quiet place, whether outside or in your home, to express your emotions to God.

# 5. MAKE IT PERSONAL

## Reflect

> I set out during the night with a few others. <u>I had not told anyone what my God had put in my heart to do for Jerusalem.</u> There were no mounts with me except the one I was riding on.
>
> Nehemiah 2:12

I remember a time when I was feeling spiritually stuck and asked an older Christian for some advice. He told me to make my relationship with God a personal one. He reminded me that we tell our closest friends things we wouldn't tell anyone else about our lives—funny things, embarrassing things, painful things, hopes, dreams, etc. He said we need to do the same thing with God and that if we don't, we will always feel a bit distant from him.

I still remember deciding that I would start sharing my deepest and most impossible dreams and hopes with God—before I told anyone else. I also decided to talk to him about doing good things, loving things, and bold things for others without looking for credit from others. When I did them, I celebrated with God and no one else. Making my relationship with God personal was one of the most powerful steps I have ever taken toward increasing my intimacy with him.

## Respond

1. How personal is your relationship with God? What can you do to increase the intimacy in your relationship?
2. What dream can you develop that will remain between you and God until he makes it clear you should share it with others?
3. What action of service, love, or boldness can you take that will remain known only to you and God—for which you will never seek praise from people?

## Act

One of the best investments you can make in your relationship with God is to purchase a journal. Use this journal for all the personal thoughts, ideas, and things you are keeping just between you and God.

## 6. TELL GOD THE TRUTH

*Reflect*

> Hear me, Lord, my plea is just; listen to my cry. Hear my prayer— it does not rise from deceitful lips. Let my vindication come from you; may your eyes see what is right. Though you probe my heart, though you examine me at night and test me, you will find that I have planned no evil; my mouth has not transgressed.
>
> Psalm 17:1–3

It is said that the most convincing lie we can tell is one we actually believe ourselves. We believe lies when we fail to regularly tell God the truth. We can increase the intimacy and security of our relationship with God by making a decision that we will never lie to God. Telling God the truth means we won't avoid, cover up, or become wilfully ignorant when we read, study, or pray. Like the psalmist, we resolve that when we are speaking to God, our mouth will not sin.

*Respond*

1. What is the most difficult truth to admit to God?
2. What is the most difficult truth to admit to yourself?
3. How do you think truth telling can increase your honesty and awareness?

*Act*

When we begin telling God the truth, we grow more secure and confident, which makes telling people the truth much easier. The action step at this point will be to identify two to three spiritual relationships (friends with whom you engage in honest and deep conversations to help each other grow in your relationship with God).

## 7. SEE YOUR SIN, FIND FORGIVENESS

*Reflect*

> Here is a trustworthy saying that deserves full acceptance: Christ Jesus came into the world to save sinners—of whom I am the worst. But for that very reason I was shown mercy so that in me, the worst of sinners, Christ Jesus might display his immense patience as an example for those who would believe in him and receive eternal life.
>
> 1 Timothy 1:15–16

Sin is probably the least popular word in religious circles these days, and yet Paul writes "a trustworthy saying that deserves full acceptance" includes the truth that he is the worst of sinners. There is no question that our sins can make us feel guilty, discouraged, and depressed. As long as we try to ignore this emotional baggage, it continues to collect in our hearts and minds.

To relieve guilt and other negative emotions related to sin, we need to see and admit them, and then trust in God's "mercy" and "immense patience"—just as Paul did. When we truly believe in God's complete forgiveness, we are reminded of how merciful he is and how much he loves us. This helps us draw close to him and develop the intimacy necessary to inspire us to choose God more and to choose sin less.

Always remember that when it comes to sin, awareness is health. The more we are aware of our sin, the more we are aware of God's love and forgiveness. The more we are aware of God's love and forgiveness, the more secure we become. The more secure we become in God, the stronger our relationships with people will be. The stronger our relationships with people are, the more comfortable we will be sharing our sins with them and helping each other overcome them (James 5:16).

**Respond**

1. How do you feel about seeing your sin every day?
2. How confident and secure are you that God forgives your sin completely?
3. How comfortable are you talking to God or people about your sins?

**Act**

One of the most important decisions we have to make is to believe in God's forgiveness, so sin doesn't make us feel that change is impossible, guilt is inevitable, and living deceptively in our relationships is unavoidable. We need to trust in God's forgiveness by studying the book of Hebrews. We should focus on seeing and appreciating the effort God has made to ensure we will be forgiven. If we really believe in God's forgiveness, we will experience an increased security in our human relationships. This security allows us to share our sins with our friends and work together with them to overcome them.

## 8. FEEL SOME EMOTION

*Reflect*

> But if serving the Lord seems undesirable to you, then choose for yourselves this day whom you will serve, whether the gods your ancestors served beyond the Euphrates, or the gods of the Amorites, in whose land you are living. <u>But as for me and my household, we will serve the Lord.</u>"

Joshua 24:15

There is something wrong in our relationship with God if it lacks passion. There is a place for duty, obedience, and being responsible—but a relationship with God that has these things and lacks passion will soon wither and die. There are few men of God in the Scriptures more passionate than Joshua. He gives one of the great speeches of the Bible when he delivers his farewell message to the nation of Israel in Joshua 24. He stands up to a nation that he believes is drifting away from God and tells them that, regardless of what they do, he will continue to dance with the one that brung him.

We must be people who can inspire others with our passion for God and, like Joshua, be able to say, "But as for me and my household, we will serve the Lord."

*Respond*

1. Which specific emotions do you feel toward God?
2. Why do you feel these particular emotions toward him?
3. How can you become more positive and passionate in your relationship with God?

## Act

The life of Joshua is one of the most exhilarating stories in all of Scripture, especially if you pay careful attention to the development of his relationship with God. Joshua didn't suddenly become passionate in his speech in Joshua 24. This passion was building up from his earliest days. Study his life by reading the book of Joshua and finding every other scripture in which he is mentioned. All along the way, make note of the people, events, and choices that made his relationship with God passionate. Make a decision to imitate his life choices so you, too, can develop this type of passionate relationship with God.

## 9. LET GOD RAISE, TRAIN, AND MATURE YOU

### Reflect

So don't feel sorry for yourselves. Or have you forgotten how good parents treat children, and that God regards you as *his* children? My dear child, don't shrug off God's discipline, but don't be crushed by it either. It's the child he loves that he disciplines; the child he embraces, he also corrects. God is educating you; that's why you must never drop out. He's treating you as dear children. This trouble you're in isn't punishment; it's *training*, the normal experience of children. Only irresponsible parents leave children to fend for themselves. Would you prefer an irresponsible God? We respect our own parents for training and not spoiling us, so why not embrace God's training so we can truly *live*? While we were children, our parents did what *seemed* best to them. But God is doing what *is* best for us, training us to live God's holy best. At the time, discipline isn't much fun. It always feels like it's going against the grain. Later, of course, it pays off handsomely, for it's the well-trained who find themselves mature in their relationship with God.

Hebrews 12:5–11, The Message

When we embrace God as a father, we have reached a significant milestone in our lives. He is no longer an entity, deity, or some other distant being. When he becomes a father, he is a parent, someone deeply involved in our lives. We experience his care and concern as well as his correction. God is no longer someone we contact, but someone whose presence is with us always. He teaches, trains, and raises us up.

## *Respond*

1. How do you feel about your parents?
2. How do you feel about God as a parent?
3. What can you do to improve your father/son or father/daughter relationship with God?

## *Act*

The first book that helped me to deepen my understanding of God as my father was *The Father Heart of God* by Floyd McClung. This book helped me see that I could draw closer to God by understanding that his love was like that of a parent. I combined those lessons with a deeper understanding of passages like Hebrews 12, which made clear to me that what I had considered God's punishment was oftentimes his parenting. Once I fully embraced God as my father, I began to see his work in every area of my life. I began to have a much less negative view of events in my life because I knew that everything God did was to raise me and help me become the best I could be.

The most important spiritual decision we make in our lives is to embrace God as a parent, trust his parenting decisions, and recognize that his love and guidance will get us exactly where we need to go.

## 10. REFLECT AND ASK YOURSELF QUESTIONS

### Reflect

<u>The person who made the idol never stops to reflect,</u> "Why, it's just a block of wood! I burned half of it for heat and used it to bake my bread and roast my meat. How can the rest of it be a god? Should I bow down to worship a piece of wood?" The poor, deluded fool feeds on ashes. He trusts something that can't help him at all. <u>Yet he cannot bring himself to ask,</u> "Is this idol that I'm holding in my hand a lie?"

Isaiah 44:19–20, NLT

One of the most enjoyable aspects of life can be reflection, especially when it is done in relationship with God. We should learn to stop, reflect, and ask ourselves questions on a regular basis. This means asking ourselves "why" questions like the ones that follow.

### Respond

1. Why do I react the way I react to God, people, or events?

2. Why do I feel the way I do about my life, circumstances, or relationships?
3. Why do I want to do what I want to do? What is my motivation?

*Act*

Learning to reflect and ask ourselves questions should be enjoyable, but it can sometimes be unpleasant. When we want to avoid certain emotions, we can find it painful to reflect and ask ourselves questions. One of the best things we can do is to reflect and ask ourselves questions in the presence of God, so that his compassion and understanding can help us make soft landings on difficult subjects.

Ecclesiastes is one of the best books to study for guidance on this type of conversation with God. It offers a number of amazing insights. One of the most overlooked is the incredible reflection and internal questioning to which Solomon subjects himself. The decision to imitate Solomon's relationship with God in this regard will have a number of transformative benefits.

## 11. GET TO KNOW YOURSELF

*Reflect*

> Those who think they know something do not yet know as they ought to know. But whoever loves God is known by God.
>
> 1 Corinthians 8:2–3

Whenever someone develops a strong relationship with God, they are going to get to know themselves better. A great many of us will consider this self-knowledge to be a benefit and a joy. There are others who will consider it difficult, resist self-discovery, and feel that internal examination is pointless navel-gazing.

As we deepen our relationship with God, we will develop more self-awareness, regardless of our disposition toward the journey. We need to accept that an important part of walking with God is being known by him. As we do this, he will reveal what he sees to us. The level of intimacy we develop in our relationship with God will depend on how receptive we are to this knowledge of ourselves. We should trust God, be secure in his love for us, and let him create in us a deeper level of understanding of ourselves, so that we can increase the intimacy of all our relationships.

### Respond

1. How do you feel about getting to know yourself better?
2. What might make you resistant to learning things about yourself?
3. In what ways can you see that God is trying to teach you things about yourself?

### Act

One of the most emotionally transformative studies we can do in Scripture on the subject of self-discovery and self-knowledge is to examine the life of King Saul in the book of 1 Samuel. This study will show you the dangers of refusing to know yourself. Think of ways you can avoid King Saul's fate.

## 12. IDENTIFY YOUR WARNING SIGNS

*Reflect*

> For God does speak—now one way, now another—though no one perceives it. In a dream, in a vision of the night, when deep sleep falls on people as they slumber in their beds, he may speak in their ears and terrify them with warnings, to turn them from wrongdoing and keep them from pride, to preserve them from the pit, their lives from perishing by the sword.
>
> Job 33:14-18

We should develop an internal list of warning signs that helps alert us when we are drifting away from God. These warning signs are usually the behaviors, circumstances, or desires we experience right before we begin to drift.

For instance, when we experience times of great discouragement, we may seek the immediate encouragement of attention from people, rather than reaching out for intimacy with God. If we recognize this warning sign, we will be alert to feelings of discouragement and make certain to reach out to God for encouragement before we turn to people. Understanding these types of warning signs will keep our relationship with God close, our relationships with people healthy, and our perspective on life wise.

*Respond*

1. When you look back on the times in your spiritual life when you drifted away from God, what patterns do you see that preceded the drifting?

2. What type of stressors do you see that can come into your life, wear you down, and eventually lead you to forget about God?
3. What signs do you see in your relationships with people right before you begin to drift away from God? For example, do you seek their attention/approval, isolate, or push them away?

*Act*

Few things are more important than becoming aware of the warning signs that you are drifting from God. Develop that list of warning signs and make a decision to stop and turn back to God whenever you see your warning signs go off.

## 13. INCREASE YOUR FAITH

*Reflect*

> We ought always to thank God for you, brothers and sisters, and rightly so, because your faith is growing more and more, and the love all of you have for one another is increasing.
>
> 2 Thessalonians 1:3

Faith and fear have an interesting relationship. The more faith we have, the less fear we feel. The more fear we feel, the less faith we have. Increasing our faith needs to be one of our greatest concerns because when our faith is increasing, our fear is decreasing.

CHAPTER EIGHT: PRACTICAL STEPS FOR MAKING GOD ATTRACTIVE

*Respond*

1. What are your five greatest fears, and how do they affect your faith?
2. What five things build your faith most quickly?
3. What can you do today to increase your faith?

*Act*

When it comes to increasing our faith, few things are as powerful as the Bible and our relationships. Two decisions that will definitely help us increase our faith are to read the Bible more consistently and to be open with our friends about our fears on a regular basis.

## 14. THINK ABOUT GOD

*Reflect*

> In his pride the wicked does not seek him; <u>in all his thoughts there is no room for God.</u>
>
> Psalm 10:4

One of the most humbling questions to answer is, "How often do you think about God?" How much we think—or fail to think—reveals more about our level of pride than almost anything else. The encouraging truth is that the more we think about God, the healthier every part of our spiritual life becomes.

*Respond*

1. How do you define "thinking about God"?
2. How often do you think about God each day?

3. How can you increase the amount of time you think about God on a daily basis?

*Act*

A revealing exercise is to compare how much we think about ourselves each day to how much we think about God. Once the comparison is made, our goal should be to make this at least a fifty-fifty split. When we increase the amount we think about God, our faith, purity of heart, and confidence all increase, along with a number of other spiritual qualities.

## 15. TALK ABOUT GOD

*Reflect*

I do not hide your righteousness in my heart; I speak of your faithfulness and your saving help. I do not conceal your love and your faithfulness from the great assembly.

Psalm 40:10

Talking about God is an indicator of humility. When we talk about God, we talk about ourselves less and give him the amount of credit he deserves. The other benefit of talking about God is that it increases the faith of our friends and family. To reduce or remove awkwardness, we need to think of creative ways to talk about him.

*Respond*

1. How often do you talk about God?
2. Where do you usually talk about God?
3. How can you increase how much you talk about God?

*Act*

Take a week and make a decision to increase the amount of time you talk about God. Be creative and discover new ways to talk about him without appearing awkward, self-righteous, or downright strange.

## 16. BUILD HEALTHY SPIRITUAL RELATIONSHIPS

*Reflect*

> And they exceeded our expectations: They <u>gave themselves first of all to the Lord</u>, and then by the will of God also to us.
>
> 2 Corinthians 8:5

Spiritual relationships are one of the most important blessings to our life and our relationship with God. At the same time, they can be one of the most tumultuous aspects of our spiritual lives. One of the keys to building great spiritual relationships is to follow the direction of 2 Corinthians 8:5 by first giving ourselves to God and then to each other. We need to make certain we are going to God first and relying on him before we turn to people. Otherwise we can become godless and preoccupied with people.

*Respond*

1. Who is the first person you go to in times of spiritual difficulty or crisis? Why is this person first?
2. How can you change your relationship with God so that you feel about him the way you do toward the person you named in question #1?

3. How can you change how you interact in your relationships so that God becomes everyone's first option, and people become second?

*Act*

The healthiest spiritual relationships are those where God is at the center. Then we are not tempted to expect more from people than is healthy. Make a decision to always keep God at the center of your spiritual relationships, so that you can have deep and close relationships with people who are spiritually healthy.

## 17. LISTEN TO LEARN WHAT OTHERS KNOW ABOUT GOD

*Reflect*

> And whenever Moses went out to the tent, all the people rose and stood at the entrances to their tents, watching Moses until he entered the tent. As Moses went into the tent, the pillar of cloud would come down and stay at the entrance, while the Lord spoke with Moses. Whenever the people saw the pillar of cloud standing at the entrance to the tent, they all stood and worshiped, each at the entrance to their tent. The Lord would speak to Moses face to face, as one speaks to a friend. Then Moses would return to the camp, but his young aide Joshua son of Nun did not leave the tent.
>
> Exodus 33:8–11

One of the fastest ways to improve our own relationship with God is to spend time with people who enjoy a great relationship with him. When we spend quiet times together with those who are close to God, we can learn new ways to make our own relationship with him more intimate.

*Respond*

1. Name five people you know who have a powerful relationship with God.
2. Make a list of five questions to ask them about improving your own relationship with God.
3. Spend some time with each of these people to learn how they read the Bible, how they pray, and how they make an emotional connection with God.

*Act*

Learning can be difficult if we are insecure or proud. We either think we already know the answer or feel embarrassed when we don't. Overcoming our need to appear knowledgeable about God is one of the first steps to learning from others how to have a great relationship with him.

## 18. USE A DIFFERENT VERSION OF THE BIBLE

*Reflect*

> They asked each other, "Were not our hearts burning within us while he talked with us on the road and opened the Scriptures to us?"
> Luke 24:32

One of the best things we can do to keep our relationship with God fresh is to read different versions of the Bible. This keeps our hearts burning rather than bored.

*Respond*

1. How do you determine which version of the Bible you read?
2. How many versions of the Bible are you aware of or have you read?
3. Do you have any aversions to using a different version? Why or why not?

*Act*

Select a new version of the Bible to use from the following list. To help you make a decision, I have added some brief descriptions.

1. **New International Version (NIV):** accurate and easy to read
2. **New American Standard Bible (NASB):** word-for-word accuracy
3. **New Living Translation (NLT):** easy to read and easy to understand
4. **New Century Version (NCV):** easy to read and easy to understand
5. **Revised English Bible (REB):** British English can be a cool change of pace
6. **New Jerusalem Bible (NJB):** poetic language
7. **The Message (Message):** fun read, but combine it with another version
8. **Amplified Bible (AMP):** fun like The Message, but more literal

## 19. USE UNCONVENTIONAL TOOLS AND METHODS

*Reflect*

They read from the Book of the Law of God, making it clear and giving the meaning so that the people understood what was being read.

Nehemiah 8:8

Technology has provided us with a number of new and creative ways to learn the Scriptures. Rather than resist these new media formats, we should give them special attention. They can be especially helpful for those who have difficulty reading.

*Respond*

1. Do you have a problem using technology rather than a traditional Bible? Why? Why not?
2. What type of technology have you used to facilitate your Bible study? What was the experience like for you?
3. Do you know anyone who could benefit from unconventional technology tools (examples are listed below) to help them in their reading and comprehension of the Bible? Who? Have you considered helping them use these unconventional tools?

*Act*

Take advantage of some of the following tools for personal use or to help someone who has reading or comprehension difficulties. Here are some of my favorites:

1. **The Bible by Tecarta**: The Tecarta Bible app works on iPhone and Android and has multiple translations.
2. **The Bible Experience Audio Bible**: This has a number of actors and celebrities reading the Bible and can be quite enjoyable.
3. **Streetlights**: This young media team brings the Bible to life through audio and print Bibles. They incorporate a modern aesthetic, employing hip hop beats to soundtrack their impassioned reading of Scripture.
4. **The Gospel of John (2003)**: A modern take on Jesus' life from the perspective of the apostle John.
5. **Deep Spirituality**: Our team has produced a series of guides, workbooks, and devotionals geared toward helping readers of all backgrounds to understand and apply the Bible.

## 20. DEVELOP A TRANSFORMATIONAL RELATIONSHIP WITH GOD

*Reflect*

But whenever anyone turns to the Lord, the veil is taken away. Now the Lord is the Spirit, and where the Spirit of the Lord is, there is freedom. And we all, who with unveiled faces contemplate the Lord's glory, are being transformed into his image with ever-increasing glory, which comes from the Lord, who is the Spirit.

2 Corinthians 3:16–18

The first step toward a transformational relationship with God is what I call a quiet time. When a person has a quiet time, they schedule a time in the morning or evening to spend time with God where they pray and read the Bible.

This quiet time is an integral part of our relationship with God. A relationship with God includes (1) a quiet time, (2) an awareness of his presence, (3) an awareness of the level of your faith, (4) an awareness of your heart condition, (5) an emotional connection with God, (6) the ability to influence daily life because of your relationship with God. The truth is that our relationship with God can only be defined as vibrant and thriving when it affects our daily lives in transformational ways. The goal is to reach beyond a quiet time to a transformational relationship with God that changes our day-to-day lives.

*Respond*

1. How strong and consistent are your quiet times?
2. How would you describe the transformational nature of your relationship with God? Have you grown beyond a basic quiet time?
3. What can you do to make your relationship with God more transformational so that it affects even greater change in your life and the lives of those you influence?

### Act

There are two major decisions to make as we go forward. The first is to have strong and consistent quiet times that increase the power and intimacy of our relationship with God. The second decision is to move our relationship with God beyond a basic quiet time to become an all-day awareness and connection with him, one that makes ongoing transformational change and growth in our lives possible.

These are just starting blocks for your journey in going deeper in your relationship with God. Don't just rush through them - take your time with them, work them into your life, and watch your relationship with God and others completely transform. It is in this daily practice of growth and depth that we can truly discover God for ourselves.

# ENDNOTES

1. "Religiosity," *Cambridge Dictionary*, Cambridge University Press, last accessed October 10, 2021, https://dictionary.cambridge.org/us/dictionary/english/religiosity.

2. Russ Ewell, "How to Discover Your Voice," Lead Different, published October 16, 2020, https://leaddiff.com/how-to-discover-your-voice/.

3. James C. Collins, *Good to Great: Why Some Companies Make the Leap ... and Others Don't* (New York: HarperCollins, 2001), p. 1. Copyright 2001 by Jim Collins. Reprinted by permission of Curtis Brown, Ltd. All rights reserved.

4. A.W. Tozer, *The Knowledge of the Holy* (New York: HarperCollins, 1961) p.4. Copyright © 1961 by Aiden Wilson Tozer. Used by permission of HarperCollins Publishers.

5. "Religion," *Merriam-Webster.com Dictionary*, Merriam-Webster, https://www.merriam-webster.com/dictionary/religion. Accessed 11 Oct. 2021.

6. "In U.S., Decline of Christianity Continues at Rapid Pace," Pew Research Center, October 17, 2019, https://www.pewforum.org/2019/10/17/in-u-s-decline-of-christianity-continues-at-rapid-pace/.

7. Christopher Hitchens, *God Is Not Great: How Religion Poisons Everything* (New York: Grand Central Publishing, 2005), 10. Copyright © 2005. Reprinted by permission of Twelve Books, an imprint of Hachette Book Group, Inc.

8. Cathy Lynn Grossman, "Survey: 72% of Millennials 'more spiritual than religious," *USA Today*, April 27 2010, https://usatoday30.usatoday.com/news/religion/2010-04-27-1Amillfaith27_ST_N.htm.

9. Henry David Thoreau, *Walden; Or, Life in the Woods*, (Boston: Tocknor and Fields, 1854).

10. Star Trek: The Original Series, "Who Mourns For Adonais," DesiLu Productions, September 22, 1967.

11. Victor Hugo, *William Shakespeare*, (Boston: Estes and Lauriat, 1864), retrieved from https://www.gutenberg.org/files/53490/53490-h/53490-h.htm#BOOK_IIIa.

12. TWO HEARTS Words and Music by BRUCE SPRINGSTEEN © 1980, 1981 BRUCE SPRINGSTEEN. All Rights Controlled and Administered by ALFRED MUSIC. All Rights Reserved. Used by Permission of ALFRED MUSIC.

13. Henry David Thoreau, *Walden; Or, Life in the Woods* (Boston: Ticknor and Fields, 1854).

14. Louis V. Gerstner, *Reinventing Education: Entrepreneurship in America's Public Schools*, (New York: Penguin Group, 1994).

15. Joel Barker, *Discovering The Future* (Ascot UK: ILI Press, 1985).

16. Copyright 1994 by Jim Collins & Jerry Porras. Reprinted by permission of Curtis Brown, Ltd. All rights reserved.

17. Anne Lamott, *Bird by Bird: Some Instructions on Writing and Life* (New York: Pantheon Books, 1994).

18. George Bernard Shaw, *Back to Methuselah, Act I, Selected Plays with Prefaces, Volume 2*, (Dodd, Mead & Company, 1949) 7. Quoted by Robert Kennedy as the theme of his 1968 presidential campaign.

19. Jesse Jackson, Address to the Democratic National Convention, July 18, 1984, https://www.pbs.org/wgbh/pages/frontline/jesse/speeches/jesse84speech.html, accessed October 2021.

20. Speech in the Assembly Hall, Paulskirche, Frankfurt, Germany, 1963.

21. Harrison Rainie, "The Most Lasting Kennedy Legacy: How Eunice Shriver and Her Family Changed The World for The Mentally Retarded," *US News & World Report* (November 15, 1993), 44.

22. Carla Baranauckas, "Eunice Kennedy Shriver, Influential Founder of Special Olympics, Dies at 88," *The New York Times* (August 11, 2009), https://www.nytimes.com/2009/08/12/us/12shriver.html.

23. Eunice Shriver, Special Olympic World Games, Indiana, USA, 1987.

24. Ibid.

25. Shriver, Tim. *Online News Hour*, NPR, KQED, July 12 2006.

26. Ibid.

27. *Meet the Press,* NBC News, August 30 2009, https://www.nbcnews.com/id/wbna32607915.

28. Toni Morrison, speech to the Ohio Arts Council, 1981.